britney
spears

Jackie Robb

HarperEntertainment
An Imprint of HarperCollins*Publishers*

HarperEntertainment
An Imprint of HarperCollins*Publishers*
10 East 53rd Street, New York, NY 10022-5299

ISBN 0-06-106620-6

First Edition 1999
Updated Edition 2000

Cover design by Susan and Jeanette

Cover photograph
©1999 Jeffrey Mayer/Star File Photo Agency, Ltd.

Printed in the United States of America

Visit HarperEntertainment on the World Wide Web at
www.harpercollins.com

❖ 1 0 9 8 7 6 5

• •

To Arthur, all my love, "One More Time"

contents

Introduction

Talented, bubbly, bright, energetic, the girl next door and then some—seventeen-year-old Britney Spears is all that and a whole lot more. She's the ultimate pop music princess, whose debut album, ...Baby One More Time, soared to the very top of the music charts. The catchy single of the same name took radio and MTV by storm, and it wasn't long before all of America was happily dancing to her tune. That song brought Britney into the limelight and turned her into an overnight "It" girl—the girl every guy wanted to get to know and every girl wanted to hang out with.

But Britney is also a down-home country girl with confidence, energy, and strong values. She may be riding in the fast-fame lane, but she's definitely remaining true to herself and her beliefs.

From Kentwood, Louisiana, to Orlando, Florida, to New York City, to the world—bouncy, bright, beautiful Britney has been mesmerizing fans with her superhuman voice and her supersweet smile. There isn't a corner of the world that wouldn't be able to sing along to the catchy chorus of "... Baby One More Time"—"My loneliness is killing me, I must confess, I still believe. . . ."

Girl singers are certainly nothing new in the pop music biz. Back in the sixties, they sang together in girl groups; in the seventies, they wailed disco tunes. But Britney is most directly descended from two lovable pop music icons of the late eighties, Debbie Gibson and Tiffany. Like them, Britney has a lovable, best-friend quality mixed with heaping helpings of talent and enthusiasm. And also like them, Britney has style and a sense of fun that appeals to fans of all ages.

But Britney's voice—her awesome, powerful, sultry, sophisticated, and ultracool voice—is what really puts her over the top! It's a voice that has been compared with those of the pop divas of our day, like Whitney Houston and Celine Dion. It's a voice that's strong, that gladly tells the world this is one singer who's arrived. It's a voice that can belt out a heart-tugging ballad or a bouncy dance tune with equal conviction and power.

And unlike those untouchable music mavens Whitney and Celine, Britney is still the type of girl you could imagine being close friends with. She's someone you'd love to chat, share secrets, shop, and giggle with, because Britney still does all those things—she's still a teenager, and that means she's always ready to have a good time doing the "girly" things she loves.

Britney may seem like an overnight sensation, but nothing could be further from the truth. She began her career back in her hometown of Kentwood, Louisiana—a seriously small town that specializes in Berry Festivals and beauty pageants. Britney started singing almost as soon as she could talk, and by the age of ten, she was already a *Star Search* Champion and local celebrity. She was also an award-winning gymnast, who spent hours a day perfecting her flips and twists—great preparation for the dance moves she would soon be known for in her hotter-than-hot videos.

At eleven, Britney was starring in the Disney Channel variety show, the *Mickey Mouse Club*, a show that launched the careers of a slew of young stars (including Britney's close buddies Justin Timberlake and J.C. Chasez of the pop-sensational singing group 'N Sync). When the show was canceled, she went back home and lived life as a "normal" teenager. For awhile, at least.

But the bright lights, the screaming fans, and the MTV cameras were out there waiting for her, and Britney was determined to have it all. She pursued her music career, and just after her seventeenth birthday she received a wonderful gift—her album soared to number one! . . . *Baby*

One More Time brought Britney into the big time.

Of course, getting there took hard work. After signing her record deal, Britney traveled the United States, appearing at local malls and bringing her music directly to her fans. Snippets of Britney songs began popping up on the Internet, whetting the appetites of listeners throughout the world. And after the release of her first single, Britney hit the road hard as the opening act for 'N Sync, a concert tour that brought her face-to-face with legions of girls— all ready, willing, and able to dance to the beat of ". . . Baby One More Time." The star herself, always modest and totally unwilling to blow her own horn, was quick to credit the power of pop music, and not her own talent.

"There was this period when everything in music was R&B," she told a popular teen magazine in one of hundreds of interviews she's done over the past year. "Then all the sudden— POP MUSIC! . . . And pop music is fun music— it puts you in a better mood. It makes you happy when you hear it. I know I feel happy when I hear a happy song I can dance and sing along to."

By early 1999, Britney was making millions of fans happy all over the world. She had quickly become one of the most beloved girl singers in pop music history. This sweet and lovely Louisiana girl, who'd always dreamed of hitting the big time with her big, big voice, was a chart-topping, platinum-selling artist. Her concerts were totally sold out, her videos were playing nonstop on MTV, and her face was popping up in magazines and on TV talk shows.

So who, exactly, is Britney Spears? How did this young girl capture the hearts of so many fans, male and female? How did she get her start? And what does her future hold? If you want the answers to these and many other questions, just sit back, get comfortable, and enjoy the read.

chapter one

A
Star Is
Born!

Britney Jean Spears made her star-studded debut in this world on December 2, 1981. Although her parents, Lynne and Jamie, already had their hands full with their lively five-year-old son, Bryan, they were delighted to welcome their dark-blond, brown-eyed daughter into the family. They spelled her first name B-r-i-t-n-e-y because, as Britney tells it, "My mom said everyone spelled it B-r-i-t-t-a-n-y, but that wasn't how it was pronounced, so she spelled it the way it sounded." They also gave their daughter the middle name of Jean, after Lynne's mother.

Lynne and Jamie brought their bundle of joy home to a Victorian-style ranch house tucked away on a quiet street in Kentwood, Louisiana, about an hour from New Orleans. With a population of 2,500, Kentwood is a place where the birth of a new baby is reason for a total town celebration. Britney remembers Kentwood as a place of simple beauty and old-fashioned goodness. It is quiet, slow-moving, and peaceful, full of serenity and grace. It has a certain old-fashioned timelessness that makes it a great place to be a kid. "It looks like something out of a movie," she told *Tiger Beat* magazine. "Everybody knows everybody. For some reason, all my mother's friends had kids at the same time, so it was like I had all these sisters."

Lynne and Jamie both worked hard to give

their kids the best life possible. Lynne was a teacher, and while baby Britney was growing up, Mom was running a day-care center. Jamie was the foreman of a construction company. When work became scarce near Kentwood, he traveled to Memphis, living there during the week and returning to spend time with his family on weekends.

Life was most excellent for baby Britney—she had a close-knit, loving family (including a big brother who constantly protected her from the world's dangers) and a slew of cousins and neighborhood girls to play with. But she wanted more.

Even at that young age, Ms. Britney Spears wanted the spotlight.

Sing-Along

From the moment she was able to talk, Britney was singing. And from the moment she was able to walk, she was flipping out! "I was crazy," Britney told *SuperTeen* magazine. "My parents' friends would come over to the house, and I would be doing flips across the room. Even then, I loved to perform." Dancing and singing were child's play for Britney, and she did both every single day.

Lynne and Jamie were astounded by their young daughter's voice—it was so strong, it sounded like it was coming from someone three times Britney's age. It was also a good voice—clear as a bell and always in perfect pitch. They encouraged Britney to indulge her love of singing.

One of the places Britney could really let her voice shine was in Sunday services. Britney and her family attended the Baptist Church every week, and she happily lent her voice to the choir. "The church has always been so important in my life," Britney told *16* magazine. "It was the center of our community. And I grew up singing there."

At the age of four, she gave her first public performance, singing "What Child Is This?" for a Christmas service. The audience—fellow parishioners—was awed by her God-given talent.

Despite her young years, Britney recognized the effect her voice had. She saw people turn their heads and listen as she sang; she watched as smiles lit up their faces. She couldn't help but realize that it was she who was making people happy—and the realization delighted her!

The giggly little girl with the voice that could light up a room started school at an early age—by the time Britney was three years old, her mother was already teaching her in the day-care center she ran. By the time Britney entered kindergarten at the Park Lane Academy in Macomb, Mississippi (about thirty minutes from her home in Kentwood), she was already reading at a level higher than her classmates. She progressed well in school—her favorite subjects were spelling and reading. But when she finished her homework at night, she always returned to her first loves, dancing and singing.

It was clear to everyone that Britney loved attention and clamored for the spotlight—but it was also clear that she had the kind of talent that made people want to watch and listen to her. Lynne began to realize that her lovely little daughter had a tremendous voice, a voice that was stronger and more melodic than that of any adult she knew. And Britney's dance moves showed grace and precision far beyond her young years.

As Britney grew, her love of music and performing grew as well. Her occasional bouts of shyness disappeared completely when she was in front of an audience. "I was always dancing in front of the TV," Britney remembers. "My mom would have company, and I'd be dancing and doing flips, and my mom's friends would say, 'Lynne, what's she doin'?' And my mom wouldn't have even noticed me, she was so used to it."

To make the most of Britney's natural gifts, her mom did what millions of parents across the country do for their daughters—she enrolled Britney in dance class. For two years, little Britney devoted herself to learning ballet, jazz, and tap and to performing in reviews and recitals. Lynne drove her daughter back and forth to class in New Orleans and was delighted to see Britney enjoying herself.

But as much fun as Britney was having, she was doing more than enjoying herself—she was dedicating herself to her dancing. She was always pushing herself to learn new steps and was always psyched to show them off once she'd perfected them.

Britney's teachers noticed that she was extremely flexible and strong—capable of doing difficult flips, cartwheels, and summersaults. They suggested to Lynne that Britney pursue gymnastics—she seemed like a natural. Britney jumped at the chance. She started taking lessons and immediately fell in love with it. Although she continued with the dance lessons (and with singing in the church choir), she began to devote herself almost entirely to gymnastics. Before long she was at the top of her class. "Doing gymnastics was so much fun," Britney remembers. "I had the best time doing those flips!"

Taking to the Beam

By the age of seven, Britney had become a serious gymnast and loved every second of it. Her father built her a beam in the middle of the living room, and Britney devoted herself to becoming the best she could be. "I used to cry if I had to miss gymnastics," Britney told *All-Stars* magazine. "My mom would drive me for an hour, one way, to get to gymnastics—she put up with that because she knew how much I loved it."

But while Britney flourished in performance gymnastics, she discovered early on that she did not enjoy the tough, sometimes harsh world of competitive gymnastics. This was particularly apparent when she traveled to Houston, Texas, to study gymnastics with the world-famous coach Bela Karolyi—the man who trained Olympic champions like Kerri Strug. "I went to a meet one time, and there were all these amazing gymnasts, so my dad suggested I try going to their gym," Britney told *16* magazine. "So I went to Bela's camp in Houston and trained there. I started working harder and harder—but by then, I was starting to cry when I had to go to gymnastics. Everyone there was so over the top. I missed the fun of it—I had been good at gymnastics because it was fun, but it got to the point where I didn't want to do it anymore."

It didn't take Britney long to realize that it was time to return to the things that made her happiest—singing and dancing. She recommitted herself to her church choir, where she continued to astound the congregation with her crystal-clear high notes. Without a trainer or anyone else to push her, Britney bloomed on her own—and her majestic voice, so clear and true, grew stronger with every note she sang. It was now evident to everyone in Britney's immediate circle of friends and family that this was one girl who needed to sing the way most kids needed to breathe.

A Regular Kid—Sort Of

If Britney was aware of her precious musical gifts, she didn't make that big a deal about them. She spent most of her spare time with her friends, being a tomboy. "My friends and I all had these go-carts," Britney told *Teen Beat*. "The thing we'd do is, we'd go to this field after it rained, and we'd go mud riding. My mom would get so mad, because we'd come home drenched in mud."

After washing off the mud, Britney would return to her baby-blue bedroom with the white bay window and play with her dolls. And as she played, she dreamed of what she'd be when she grew up. The dream was always the same—she wanted to sing for millions of people and make the whole world smile! She had no idea that in a very short time, her dreams would be "this close" to coming true.

gettin'
It Started

By the time she reached her eighth birthday, Britney knew she wanted to pursue a life in music. The question was how to begin. That definitely was not an easy question for a kid from Kentwood, Louisiana, to answer!

Luckily, Britney didn't have to come up with the answer herself—it came to her in the form of another Brit, one of Britney's closest friends from gymnastics. "Brittany's mom had heard about an open call audition for something called the *Mickey Mouse Club*," Britney told *Teen Machine*. The two Brits begged their moms to drive to Atlanta, where the casting call was being held.

An open casting call for young performers means total pandemonium, and that's just what the girls faced at the studio in Atlanta where the auditions were being held. Hundreds of girls and boys between the ages of ten and seventeen had turned up; many had driven thousands of miles from all over the South. The *Mickey Mouse Club*, which had already been on the air for several years and was a seriously popular show for the Disney Channel, was just the type of opportunity a young performer needed to break into the big time. The show gave its young stars the chance to sing, dance, act in skits, and even do comedy sketches. Britney knew this was where she belonged, and she was determined to make the cut.

She did very well on her first audition—

well enough to make it right down to the wire as one of that day's finalists. At the end of the day, Britney was poised to nab a spot on the *Mickey Mouse Club*. But it was not to be—not this time around at least. "The producers thought I was still too young," Britney told *SuperStars*. "I was so disappointed, I couldn't believe it!"

The producers of the *Mickey Mouse Club* knew that eight-year-old Britney was still too little to keep up with the grueling demands of the show schedule—the youngest cast members at that time were ten and eleven— but they also knew talent when they saw it, and they definitely saw it in Britney Spears. They were not about to let this catch get away.

The producers sat down with Britney and Lynne and began to map out a game plan for Britney's future. First stop, they decreed, must be New York City. They knew of an agent and an entertainment lawyer there who could help Britney take her first baby steps into showbiz.

Lynne was totally floored by the prospect. New York City? What a completely crazy idea! "Where I'm from, you just don't say, 'I'm going to New York,'" Britney told *SuperTeen*. "People were like, 'What are you doing?' It was totally unheard of." So Lynne took her talented daughter back home to Kentwood.

But Britney couldn't stop thinking about New York City and the promise of a music career. Although she continued performing in local talent shows and in the church choir, she felt completely ready to become a show business professional. She kept after her parents, who eventually gave in to their strong-willed and determined child. "I was like, please, Mom, take me! I wanted to go to New York so bad. So I just kept asking my mom and dad, and they believed in me enough to do it. I really wanted to do it, and I was so thankful because they were so supportive. I think they both knew I had this in me," Britney told America Online.

That summer, Lynne and Britney packed their bags and, leaving Jamie and Bryan behind, flew off to the Big Apple. It was their first time in such an enormous, daunting city. It took a while for them to adjust to it. "I thought I was never going to get used to it," Britney remembers. "I was so scared when I first got there. It was like another world to me." But the newness wore off, and soon it was a world young Britney had become very comfortable in.

She's Gonna Live Forever!

Like the characters in the movie *Fame*, Britney began to work full time on her craft. For three summers in a row, she studied at the Professional Performing Arts School (*Home Alone* actor Macaulay Culkin is an alumnus) and at the Dance Center, a well-known Off-

Broadway organization devoted to dance instruction and the arts. Britney and her mom lived in a small New York City apartment, and the family reunited for weekend visits whenever possible.

Although she was still only eight years old, Britney devoted herself to her studies and training. It wasn't long before she made her mark on New York—and as the song says, if you can make it there, you'll make it anywhere.

Britney's big-time dreams finally started to come true when she made it to Off-Broadway. In 1991, she auditioned for and won a role in a comedy called *Ruthless,* based on the 1956 horror film *The Bad Seed.* Britney played Tina, the sweet-faced young thing who is really a ruthless killer run amuck. "It was the hardest thing I've ever done," Britney told *Tiger Beat.* "I was playing the main role, and it was every single night. Plus I was keeping up with my studies. I was really working hard." But for Britney, the payoff was definitely worth it— applause from a live audience. "The show was about this little girl who's really evil," Britney remembers. "I was the little girl—I killed my best friend in the show! It was funny, but in a really sick way. Everybody really seemed to love it."

During that busy time, Britney also worked in commercials, appearing in TV ads for Mitsubishi cars and Malls barbecue sauce, as well as in countless regional commercials. Again she wowed everyone with her professionalism and her talent.

The two years Britney spent working in New York provided her with one of the best learning experiences she could have had, but after six months of working on *Ruthless,* she decided she was ready to pack it in and head home for awhile. "It was Christmas, and I wanted to go home, so I went home," she told *16* magazine.

Oh, Baby, Baby!

Britney returned home to a new role—one she hadn't been preparing for but that she was very excited about: that of big sister. There was a brand-new family addition she was dying to get to know—little Jamie Lyn had been born while Britney was away, and Britney could hardly wait to greet her new sibling. "I always loved taking care of Jamie Lyn," Britney told *Teen Beat.* "It was almost like she was my child, because there's a ten-year age difference, and I always felt protective of her."

After Britney settled in at home and started taking her regular classes at Park Lane Academy, she began attending to some practical matters—like getting a dreaded retainer, a prelude to the braces she later wore. "That retainer was the ugliest thing," she told *16* magazine. "It was like this red thing and had a metallic bottom, and it had a key I had to turn every night, that made the retainer tighter. I lost that thing so many times! I remember I lost it in the cafeteria at school, and it got thrown away—and they dug it out of the garbage can! Later on, when I actually got my braces, I thought they were cool—like I was a real teenager with my metal mouth! But that retainer, that was just gross!"

She's a Star

Although she had just spent two years working in New York City, it would be her home state of Louisiana that would bring Britney her real big break. The long-running TV show *Star Search* was auditioning talent in Baton Rouge, Louisiana, and Britney convinced her mom to take her down. Of course, the show's producers were wowed by Britney's big voice, and she nabbed a spot on the nationally televised show. Lynne left the baby and Bryan with Jamie while she and Britney traveled to Los Angeles, where the show was filmed. Britney was a Junior Vocalist contestant. For the first time, she would be presenting herself and her talent to an audience that numbered in the millions.

Britney, all dolled up in a little black dress with a white lace collar and a huge bow in her blondish-brown curls ("I couldn't believe my mama dressed me up in that outfit!" she told *All-Stars* magazine), had the crowd eating out of her hand as she performed her song. They could hardly believe that enormous, powerful voice was coming out of such a tiny ten-year-old.

The judges agreed that Brit was a singing sensation, and she won her first competition. Unfortunately, the following week she lost the title. But Britney was still a big winner in the eyes of all who heard her singing her heart out. No one who heard her sing would ever forget her.

And Britney would certainly never forget the thrill of performing on TV for a national audience. In fact, the experience got her thinking about a certain Club she still wanted to join!

Aged to Perfection

It was just a few weeks before her eleventh birthday, and Britney was thinking about the *Mickey Mouse Club* again. After all, it had been two whole years since her first audition, and she'd certainly learned a lot since then. She'd starred on the New York stage, and even appeared on (and won) *Star Search*. Perhaps she should take another chance and audition again.

The *Mickey Mouse Club's* producers had not forgotten Britney, and when she auditioned for the show's 1993 TV season, there was no way they were going to let her go again. This bundle of talent was more than ready to face the TV lights and cameras, as well as the live audience that came to cheer on the *Mickey Mouse Club* cast each week. Britney got the job, and once again her mom packed their bags. They moved into a small apartment in Orlando, Florida, not far from Disney's MGM Studios theme park—close enough, in fact, that Lynne could walk her daughter to work every morning! For the next two years, Britney lived her dream—she was a full-fledged member of the Club. There was no stopping her now!

chapter three

Club Kid

Britney had craved to be a part of the *Mickey Mouse Club* since she was eight years old, and by the time she was eleven, she was ready to grab a pair of Mickey Mouse ears of her own! By the time Britney became a Mouseketeer (as the Club members were called), the show was already entering its sixth season as one of the Disney Channel's top attractions. It was filmed in front of a live audience at Disney World's MGM Studios, so Britney got to entertain people face-to-face.

The show first aired in 1988, and its concept was simple, fun, and truly entertaining. The premise? Twenty young people, aged eleven to nineteen, from all across America, sing, dance, act in comedy skits, and introduce famous guest stars. The wild and wacky aspect of the show was complemented by a more serious, socially conscious side. Each episode focused on issues that were important to teens, like just saying no to drugs or resisting peer pressure.

Each *Mickey Mouse Club* episode was divided into sections. There was Music Day, where singers like Shai and Brian McKnight would perform. There was Guest Day, where a member of the Club would visit a celeb like Tatyana Ali from *The Fresh Prince of Bel Air* or Jonathan Taylor Thomas from *Home Improvement*. Hall of Fame Day spotlighted the outstanding achievements of everyday kids.

Party Day allowed the Mouseketeers to celebrate special days with themed parties. And What I Wanna Be/See provided viewers with an opportunity to explore career choices and travel to exotic lands. The concept was a hit, and so were the show's talented teenage stars. Audiences tuned in every day to catch a glimpse of the energetic and appealing performers.

In addition to the show, there was also a popular *Mickey Mouse Club* album, which debuted in 1993—the year Britney jumped on board. The album featured twelve original songs by thirteen of the Mouseketeers, and the group planned a ten-city concert tour to publicize their music, which was a mix of R&B, funk, and hip-hop.

Earning Her Ears

Britney debuted on the *Mickey Mouse Club* along with six other newcomers: Christina Aguilera, Nikki DeLoach, T.J. Fantini, Ryan Gosling, Tate Lynche, and Justin Timberlake. (If some of those names sound familiar, there's good reason—check out the enormously successful alumni of the show in the next chapter.)

Britney began to split her time between her home in Kentwood and her new home in Orlando. She also began to train with the show's vocal coach to strengthen her voice and prepare for the arduous schedule of a variety show. "It was a great training ground," Britney told *16* magazine. "We were all like a family. We were all different ages—like from twelve to twenty—and we were all singing and dancing and acting. It was the greatest experience."

The *Mickey Mouse Club* also gave Britney her first taste of national exposure and publicity. As soon as she began appearing on the show she started receiving tons of fan mail, and she began popping up in a variety of magazines for young readers. Her fans learned that (back then) her nickname was Bit-Bit, that she loved Tom Cruise, vanilla ice cream, and the book *Little Women,* and that she had no use for selfish people. She was quoted as saying, "Life is short, don't waste it," and urged fans to "be kind and respectful of others."

Although Britney was still young, she immediately took to performing in front of a live audience again. Her years of gymnastics, singing competitions, and Off-Broadway performances had given her poise and confidence on stage, and she was perfectly comfortable doing anything the script called for, from taking a pratfall in a skit to belting out solos. At a young age, Britney already exhibited the signs of a showbiz professional, ready to learn new things and eager to show off her skills.

She wasn't too professional to play, though! Britney was fascinated by the heavy makeup applied to her face (necessary when you're performing under bright lights). So fascinated, in fact, that she wanted to wear it all the time. "I used to put it on after the show was done filming and ask everyone, 'Do you like my makeup?'" Britney told *Teen Beat.* "I cried when everyone told me I was too young to wear it every day!"

Britney and the rest of the cast also found plenty of fun things to do during their free time—after all, the studio was right in the center of Disney World! "We had such fun in those theme parks," Britney remembers. "It was like living and working in a fantasy world!"

Working for a Living

Life as a Mouseketeer might have been fun for Britney, but it wasn't always easy. The team worked Tuesday through Saturday—as in *all day* Tuesday through Saturday. Britney would wake up at 7 A.M. and catch the van that drove her and her fellow cast members to their special school on the show's back lot. From 9 A.M. to 12:30 P.M., they were tutored (Britney was an ace in social studies and English, but she had to struggle through math class, which she was never particularly crazy about). After school came rehearsals, which would run anywhere from one to three hours, depending on the script and how quickly everyone learned it. Hair, wardrobe, and makeup followed, and by 3:45 P.M., Britney was ready to go on. The show would then be taped—three hours of nonstop performing in front of an audience. After the taping, Britney would head home to eat dinner and do her homework. It was a grueling schedule, but she took to it like a fish to water. "I was learning exactly how much I loved performing," she told *Teen Beat* magazine. "That was when I realized how much I loved to sing."

Since Britney was the youngest Mouseketeer (along with Christina Aguilera—the two became best friends for the two years they appeared on the show), she admits that she had it a little easier than some of the older kids, who probably felt a lot more pressured to be perfect in front of the camera. "I was the baby," Britney told America Online. "I was eleven, the youngest one on the show, so people catered to me. And goodness, being in Disney World alone was so much fun for me. It was like a dream come true."

The friendships that were formed during the time Brit spent on the *Mickey Mouse Club* were intense, so it's no surprise that when Britney remembers the old days, she sounds just a little sad about losing touch with so many of her old friends. "I hope we all have a reunion some day," she told *Tiger Beat* magazine. "It would be a shame, you know, to think about never seeing those people again. The bonds between us were so strong."

And what about the big rumor surrounding Britney's "young love" with fellow *MMCer*

Justin Timberlake? The two were just eleven when they met and became friends, and they definitely shared some sweet hand-holding moments (and even an innocent smooch or two). But they were not serious. In fact, Justin's real first girlfriend was another cast member named Mindy.

For Britney, her time at the *Mickey Mouse Club* gave her two very important gifts. The first was the experience of a lifetime—the chance to learn new skills and perfect her old ones. The second was proof once again that a life in the spotlight was what she most craved.

Two years after Britney signed on with *MMC*, the show was canceled. And although everyone on the show was disappointed, it would be, for Britney, a major turning point. "After *Mickey Mouse Club*, I decided to go back home to Kentwood and try to just be a regular kid," Britney told *Teen Machine*. But those "regular kid" days would most certainly not last forever.

Britney's *MMC* Stats

One of the many things Britney learned from being on TV was that the audience wants to know everything! Teen magazines were constantly interviewing the young cast of *Mickey Mouse Club*, and Britney was no exception.

Although she was young, Britney had

already developed some strong opinions and definite tastes—and she was completely comfortable about sharing them with everyone. She filled out a fact sheet back in 1993 on which she listed her favorite things.

1. **Color:** *Blue*
2. **TV Show:** *Home Improvement*
3. **Movie:** *The Hand That Rocks The Cradle*
4. **Actors:** *Tom Cruise and Demi Moore*
5. **Singers:** *Whitney Houston*
6. **Food:** *Pizza*
7. **Book:** *Little Women*
8. **Vacation Spot:** *Florida*
9. **Sports Team:** *Chicago Bulls*
10. **Best Day Of Her Life:** *"When I found out I had gotten the Mickey Mouse Club."*

chapter four

The Mickey Mouse Club Hall of Fame

Britney Spears is just one of the *Mickey Mouse Club* alumni whose career really took off after the show ended. A whole bunch of Britney's co-Mouseketeers are currently making names for themselves in different areas of the entertainment world. Check them out.

KERI RUSSELL: *Mickey Mouse Club*'s golden girl, Keri Russell has taken her long mane of dark blond curls and her sweet, sincere smile to the top of the ladder in television. After starring in a short-lived NBC show called *Malibu Shores* in 1996 (a show that was created by *90210*'s Aaron Spelling), Keri soared to superstardom as the lead in a show of her very own, *Felicity*. The show was hyped in a big way months before it hit the airwaves, and when it did, it became clear that Keri had that something special that spells superstar. In January of 1998, Keri won a Golden Globe Award for Best Actress in a TV Drama.

TONY LUCCA: Keri's *MMC* co-star became her *Malibu Shores* co-star—and all the while, the two were a very together, in-love couple. (They'd started dating during their *MMC* days, proving that young love can last!) These days, Tony's staying away from the harsh glare of the TV lights and working on his music—he's a talented singer, musician, and songwriter whose CD can be purchased over the Internet. The pair live together in an apartment in California and are totally happy.

NIKKI DELOACH: Born and raised in Georgia, Nikki grew up singing and was determined to pursue a musical career after leaving *MMC*. She is currently a member of the girl group Innosense (a group Britney almost joined as well). Their debut album will be in record stores soon.

RHONA BENNETT: The gal who hailed from Chicago, Illinois, and wowed audiences with her awesome voice is currently working on her debut album.

RYAN GOSLING: The sweet blond boy with the impish but innocent smile showed up recently on the syndicated hit TV show *Young Hercules*. The show films in New Zealand, so Ryan was away when his former *Mickey Mouse Club* co-star Britney hit it huge. "I knew she was destined for great things," he told *16* magazine.

JOSH ACKERMAN: The bright-eyed, sarcastic, and lovable comedian of the Club, Josh is currently working on his first love, music.

CHRISTINA AGUILERA: One of Britney's closest friends on the Club, Christina shared Brit's ambition and love of music. She recorded the song "Reflections" for the *Mulan* soundtrack and is currently awaiting the release of her own pop album.

J. C. CHASEZ and **JUSTIN TIMBERLAKE:** The boys are all right and in sync—as in 'N Sync! Justin and J.C. kept in contact after the cancellation of the *Mickey Mouse Club*, and both continued to work on their vocal abilities and dancing techniques. In 1997, when pop music was just beginning to hit its peak again, the guys hooked up with Chris Kirkpatrick, Joey Fatone, and Lance Bass, and the rest is 'N Sync history! J.C. remembers his *Mickey Mouse Club* years with pride. He told *Teen Beat* magazine, "It was the greatest experience, because we all got to do so many things. We sang, we danced, we acted—we even did comedy skits. It taught me so much about performing. Doing a variety show like that was the best experience I could have had. It prepared me for all the hard work and performing that's involved in the music business. I know I'm a better entertainer because of my years on *MMC*." And as for Justin—who, like Britney, was one of the "babies" on the show—he simply remembers, "It was a great time, and I'll never forget a second of it."

In hindsight, the *Mickey Mouse Club* was an amazing show that gave many talented young people the chance to shine for the first time—and obviously not the last. But Britney told *Teen Machine* that she never dreamed she and her co-Mouseketeers would reach such heights of fame. "I was twelve years old then, and it was a total friend thing for me, for everybody," she says. "We never really thought, 'Oh, this person is going to do this, or that person is going to do that.' No one ever said that. We would say, 'I wish you the best of luck' and everything, but we never sat around discussing where we would end up. So it's weird to look back and see how well everyone's done. It's just amazing to think about where we started and where we all are now."

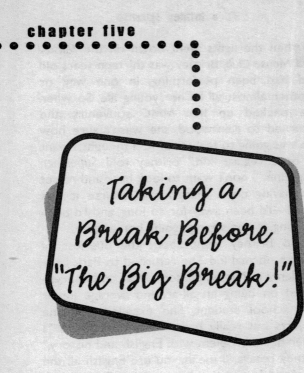

chapter five

Taking a
Break Before
"The Big Break!"

When the lights went down on the *Mickey Mouse Club,* Britney was thirteen years old and had been performing, in one way or another, almost all of her young life. So when she packed up her *MMC* souvenirs and returned to Kentwood, she wasn't sure how she was going to feel about it. "I thought, I want to be a regular kid," Britney told *SuperTeen* magazine. "I don't want to look back and regret not having done that. But of course it was weird—I'd been away for so long, and I'd been working. It was strange going home again."

So Britney went about the business of being a normal kid. She returned to Park Lane Academy in Mississippi for a year and concentrated on being an all-around average junior high school student. She excelled in some subjects but really had to work at others. "I never had a problem with English and history," Britney recalls. "I mean, you use English all the time, and history is so interesting. But math— no way. I was a total goob at it." Britney also enjoyed the "regular girl" activities she and her friends did as often as possible—going to the movies, shopping, and just hanging out. She also loafed a little. "At home, I could get away with doing nothing," she told a local New Orleans newspaper. "I'd come home from school, watch TV. In the summer, I lay out by the pool." Britney also dated occasionally, and she gossiped with her friends about boys she liked.

The one activity that Britney didn't participate in? Talking on the phone! "I'm not a phone person," she told *16* magazine. "My friends love talking on the phone all day—they'll call me up and ask, 'What are you doin'? What are you watching on TV?' Me, I'd rather talk to someone in person!"

Occasionally, of course, Britney got herself into some trouble. "When I started going out with my girlfriends, my mom would give me a curfew," Britney told *Teen Beat.* "I always thought it was too early! But my dad was always stricter than my mom. One time I remember, there was this guy I really liked. I went to stay at my friend's house, and he came over and we rode into town for awhile. It was my way of getting to go out with him! But when my dad picked me up the next morning he was really angry, and I got punished for that. But it wasn't too bad—I mean, if my parents punished me by taking away the phone, I'd be like, 'OK, I'm not on the phone anyway!'"

In other words, Britney lived a totally normal life.

But after a few months of the normal life, she started to come to some serious realizations. She saw that the normal teenage rites of passage were great, but she still longed for the spotlight. Although she loved spending time with her friends and family, she missed the excitement of working and performing every day. And while she enjoyed sharing secrets with her friends, she found it hard to convey to them just what performing meant to her. Most importantly, she was coming to understand that show business was, to her, more than a childhood hobby—it was a calling, a career that she was destined for, charged by an ambition that was in her blood. "I wasn't happy just hanging around at home," she told *Tiger Beat* magazine. "I wanted to see the world and make music and do all these wonderful things."

Almost Innosense

Around that same time, Britney got word that a girl group was forming down in Orlando, Florida. Nikki DeLoach, her *MMC* co-star and close friend, had already signed on, and Britney was asked if she wanted to try out for it as well. The group would be called Innosense. "I thought it would be a lot of fun to be in a girl group with Nikki," Britney told *16* magazine.

She auditioned in the months just before her fifteenth birthday, and she did very well, but she eventually realized it wasn't for her. "I decided not to do it," she remembers. "The timing was just wrong, because I was still going through my 'regular kid' phase." (The group Innosense did get a record deal, by the way. The girls—Nikki, Mandy Ashford, Danay Ferrer, and Veronica Finn—are managed by Lynn Harless, who happens to be the mom of 'N Sync's Justin Timberlake. Got it?)

The "almost" experience with Innosense, along with her own overwhelming determination to return to the performing life, led Britney to make some serious life-altering decisions. She came to the conclusion that a girl group was not the answer for her—for Britney, it would be a solo career, all the way to the top! "I suddenly realized that's what I wanted," she told *SuperStars* magazine. "And suddenly everything became clear."

Britney ended her high school career and enrolled in a home school program based out of the University of Nebraska. "It's mainly for kids who travel with their parents, who are missionaries," she told *All-Stars* magazine. "I took the prep course, and it was so over my head. I had to get one of my teachers to come and help me, and my answers on the prep test were still wrong. It was so hard, oh my goodness!"

But the home schooling was necessary because Britney was on a musical mission, and she definitely didn't have time to do the regular school grind. She was busy every day, preparing demo tapes she would eventually send to Jive Records, the company that signed her. Every single afternoon she would sing into her tape recorder, dreaming of the time when she could use that tape to get a record deal of her own.

Although Britney would never regret taking a year off to pursue a normal teenage life, she admits that for her it got old very quickly. "I got really, really bored," she told *Teen Machine*. "I just wanted to perform again." Britney would get her wish, but it would take a lot of work and a lot of determination—and fifteen-year-old Britney was totally ready for it.

chapter six

Time to Make the Music

All the years of working within the entertainment industry paid off for Britney when she decided to pursue her solo music career because she knew exactly how to go about it. The question remained: Was the world ready for her powerful pipes and over-the-top energy?

The answer would prove to be a resounding yes! By the time Britney made her move, pop music—the kind Britney loved and wanted desperately to make—was high on the charts again. Grunge, alternative, and rap music had dominated the charts for years, but now peppy pop tunes—like those sung by Hanson, the Spice Girls, and the Backstreet Boys—were returning to radio in a big way. The timing could not have been better.

And that's what Britney's entertainment lawyer, Larry Rudolph, told her dad when the two first talked about building a career for Britney. (Larry had known Britney since her days in New York City.) "Larry told my father that pop music was coming back," Britney told *Entertainment Weekly.* "He told me to make a tape and send it to him."

Britney gathered up the precious demo tape she'd been recording, put it into an envelope along with a photo of herself, and sent it on to Larry—who knew immediately that Britney had the talent to make it to the top. He could see she had a great look, and after listening to the demo tape, he knew she had the perfect sound. He brought the tape and the picture to Jive Records in New York City. Everyone at Jive agreed—this girl had it goin' on!

But the tape was only an introduction—the executives at Jive needed to meet Britney to make sure she could really sing, that the tape they'd heard didn't use technical tricks to enhance her soulful voice. Soon Britney was back in the Big Apple to audition in person for the creative staff at Jive Records. "I went there with this dinky little tape," she told *Billboard* magazine. "I felt so weird, standing in a conference room, basically singing for my life. But you have to take whatever opportunities come your way and make the most of them."

As usual, Britney made the most of her golden opportunity. She sang her heart out, and again her audience—this time made up of record executives—couldn't believe what they heard. They signed Britney immediately. She was ecstatic. "I thought, this was too good to be true!" she told *Entertainment Weekly*.

Jive's Talkin'

Teaming up with Jive Records was the smartest thing Britney could possibly have done. The label had built a strong reputation guiding the career of the Backstreet Boys: It had spent well over three years putting together the group's awesome self-titled debut CD, which had reached platinum seven times around the world. Jive Records was the company that had helped Kevin Richardson, Howie Dorough, Brian Littrell, A.J. McLean, and Nick Carter become international superstars, and they were certainly in a position to help Britney achieve the same success.

Jive Records' senior vice president of Artists & Repertoire, Jeff Fenster, was confident that Britney had the right stuff. "Her vocal ability caught me right away," he told *Billboard* magazine. Now it was his job to team Britney up with producers and writers who could use that vocal ability to make the most beautiful music imaginable.

The Sweep to Sweden

Although those outside the pop music world might not know it, Sweden has become an international mecca for recording studios. The pop group 'N Sync recorded their debut album there, and the Backstreet Boys did some work there as well. It was decided that Britney would record most of her album there, then return to New York to work on postproduction.

Britney flew to Sweden to meet with legendary producer and writer Eric Foster White, who'd created musical magic for artists like Boyzone and Whitney Houston. Together with Sweden's Cheiron Productions team— producer Max Martin (who'd worked extensively with the Backstreet Boys) and Per

Magnusson—Eric wrote the songs that would appear on ... *Baby One More Time*.

Jive's Jeff Fenster took the trip with Britney, and together the entire creative team began working on the album. Everyone was impressed with how quickly the recording sessions sped by—most of it was finished in an astounding ten days. "They came up with such incredible stuff," Jeff told *Billboard* magazine. "It came together so quickly for a pop album. It was a case of good chemistry among a group of very talented people."

Britney was especially psyched when she realized that most of the recording would take place in the studio Eric Foster White had built in his own home. "It was so comfortable," she told *16* magazine. "It was hard work, but we always took the time to goof around and act stupid." That comfort level was important to Britney, who was confident, but nervous about working with such major music players.

Getting Inspired

The star-to-be was caught in a total whirlwind of work—every day she went into the studio and gave her music everything she had. Every night she went home and fell soundly asleep. Although the experience was intense, it energized her. Working with such talented writers inspired her to write her own songs—something she'd never done before.

Although Britney did not write any of the songs on her first album, she hopes some of her tunes will appear on future records. In fact, the very first song she wrote, "I'm So Curious," will be on the B-side of her next single. It's a song she loves—and you'll never guess how she wrote it! "I don't really have time to sit down and write," she told *Tiger Beat* magazine. "But when I think of a melody, I call up my answering machine and sing it, so I won't forget it. Then I press play and hear myself singing the song!"

New York Bound

After putting down her vocal tracks, Britney got back on a plane and returned to New York, where the final recording sessions took place. She was thrilled to be back in the Big Apple. "Every time I'm away, I just can't wait to be back," said Britney of her adopted hometown. "I love being in the city—although the taxi drivers make me nervous. When I'm in the backseat of a taxi, I just close my eyes!"

While the final work was being done on the album, Britney got a chance to enjoy herself. She indulged in her love of Southern food, eating at Virgil's Restaurant ("It's got the best cheese grits!"); she shopped and attended dance class regularly. She quickly got used to the frantic city pace and fell in love with it. Country girl Britney was slowly becoming a citizen of the world. New York City would be just the beginning.

Ready or Not!

In mid-1998, everyone involved with Britney's debut album gave it a listen and realized they had a serious hit on their hands. But recording the album was simple compared with what came next—getting people to listen to it by promoting it around the world. Was Britney up to the challenge?

chapter seven

Jet-Setting
the World
on Fire

In June of 1998, the world got its first earful of pop princess Britney Spears—and everyone loved what they heard!

To build momentum and generate media interest and public awareness of the CD, Jive Records carefully put together a plan to get the word out about Britney's debut album.

The first thing the record company did was set up a toll-free number so that both established and potential fans could call in and listen to snippets of the music as well as to interviews with the star herself. They put the telephone number on a series of postcards, which were then sent to members of other pop music artists' fan clubs, such as the Backstreet Boys Fan Club. The promotion worked like a charm—people who called in to hear Britney's music were intrigued. They couldn't wait to hear more.

Next, Jive Records jumped into cyberland. They set up a World Wide Web Page that featured pictures, interviews, and even more music clips. Fans in the United States were just beginning to get to know Britney, and the response was enthusiastic. They seemed especially taken with the catchy, not-to-be-forgotten "... Baby One More Time," which was slated to be Britney's first single. "People seemed to really love that song," Britney told

Teen Beat. "Everyone thought that one was going to do really well."

Flying Far and Wide

If Britney thought she could take a rest after recording the CD, she was mistaken. The time had come for the really hard work!

To promote her album, Britney flew to Singapore. That might seem to be an odd choice for a young pop artist's first promotional concert, but in actuality it was a smart one. Singapore—all of Asia, really—is extremely open to popular music and totally into American culture, so it was the perfect place to launch Britney-mania.

Britney gave her first live concert there and came away from it invigorated and excited. The audiences screamed out her name and danced along to her music—even though many were hearing it for the first time! They loved Britney, and she returned that sentiment. "Oh my goodness, I was so nervous, because it was my first perfor mance," she told *Teen Machine* magazine. "But it was nice. Such a beautiful place. It was so hot outside—it was so muggy, you had to take five showers a day. But it was just perfect. The people and the country were beautiful." To this day, Britney names Singapore as one of her favorite places in the world—she especially loved the shopping! Performing in

Singapore marked a brilliant beginning to what was turning into a brilliant career. Britney had proved she could take the world by storm—but could she hold her own in her own backyard?

chapter eight

Hittin'
the Road

Britney returned to the United States after her exciting concert appearances in Singapore and immediately began another road trip—the homegrown kind! Three months before the release of the single ". . . Baby One More Time," Britney began an intense mall tour of middle America. With two dancers to back her up (and to help her pass out free cassette samplers to all in attendance), Britney set off on a twenty-eight-day jaunt that was sponsored by *YM, Teen, Seventeen,* and *Teen People* magazines. But before she could start her trip, there was one last thing she needed to do.

Her mom, Lynne, had been doing a lot of the traveling with Britney. But they had been told that the upcoming months would be grueling, and Lynne felt she couldn't go out on the road with little Jamie Lyn, who'd just turned seven. "It wasn't fair to make a seven-year-old travel around the world and not have a normal life," Britney told *SuperStars* magazine. "My mom knew she had to stay home and take care of Jamie Lyn, so we had to come up with a plan."

Enter Felicia Culotta, a close friend of Lynn's. "I had moved to New York and was a nanny," Felicia explained to *16* magazine. "After I'd been working at the same place for two years, I figured it was time for a change, and on the very weekend I made that decision, Lynne came to New York with Britney for a meeting with the record company. We all had dinner together, and Lynne said, 'We have a proposition for you! We need someone to take care of Britney.' So it all worked out perfectly!" Felicia took on the responsibility and started traveling with Britney as her guardian. (Lots of fans already know Felicia—she plays the teacher in Britney's ". . . Baby One More Time" video, and she's at absolutely every concert and public appearance.)

With Felicia in place as her caretaker, Britney was ready to hit the road, and hit the malls!

Shop 'n' Sing

Britney's mall tour was a smashing success in every way. As she toured throughout the Midwest, she got a chance to perfect her stage show, integrating precise, eye-catching choreography with her pumped-up pop sound. She also learned a lot about the intensity of a bus tour—the long hours, the lack of sleep, endless movies on the VCR, and days away from home and family. "The only downside to all this is being away from your family," Britney told *Teen Beat* magazine. "Luckily my family is so close, we really bond." To beat the homesick blues, Britney stayed plugged in to her cell phone, which never leaves her side. "I don't even want to know how much money I spent on phone calls home!" she says. "I just call up my mom

Britney performing at a *YM*
magazine charity concert in
Los Angeles . . . and
enjoying a quiet moment
by herself later.
(©1999 Vinnie Zuffante/Star File
Photo Agency, Ltd.)

The reigning queen of pop in Japan, where she was promoting her debut album.
(©1999 Todd Kaplan/Star File Photo Agency, Ltd.)

Britney sneaking a peek at the sights during her tour of Tokyo and Osaka.

(©1999 Todd Kaplan/Star File Photo Agency, Ltd.)

Too many awards for just two hands to hold!
(©1999 V.D.I./Star File Photo Agency, Ltd.)

Dressed to the nines, Britney attends the MTV European Music Awards in Ireland.
(©1999 V.D.I./Star File Photo Agency, Ltd.)

Britney serving up an
ace performance at
the US Open . . .
(©1999 Todd Kaplan/
Star File Photo
Agency, Ltd.)

. . . and flashing a
winning smile for the
cameras at a Z-100
promotional event
in New York.
(©1999 Todd Kaplan/
Star File Photo Agency, Ltd.)

Britney warms up while her dancers strike a pose.
(©1999 Jeffrey Mayer/Star File Photo Agency, Ltd.)

Taking time out with friends from 98° at the Z-100
Zootopia concert in New York.
(©1999 Todd Kaplan/Star File Photo Agency, Ltd.)

Britney smiles for the cameras with her mom—or is that her sister? (©1999 Vinnie Zuffante/Star File Photo Agency, Ltd.)

Responding to fan mail is one of her favorite things to do . . . (©1999 Todd Kaplan/Star File Photo Agency, Ltd.)

. . . that is, when she's not singing! (©1999 Jeffrey Mayer/Star File Photo Agency, Ltd.)

Britney pleasing the crowds at the KIIS-FM Radio
Show at Dodger Stadium in Los Angeles.
(©1999 Jeffrey Mayer/Star File Photo Agency, Ltd.)

and say, 'Mama, what are you doin'?' I don't care what time of day it is, I just want to hear her voice."

Of course the mall tour had one or two embarrassing moments along the way. One major one still makes Britney laugh and blush. "The thing was, I was getting ready to perform '. . . Baby One More Time,' which was the last song," she told *Tiger Beat* magazine. "And I was on the stage, and my headset fell off, which is not good at all. Then, another time, I have this big costume I wear at the beginning of the show, where I look like one of the dancers. It's got Velcro on it, and when I start singing it comes off, and I have my performing costume on underneath. Well one day, it decides not to come off! I'm stuck in there, and the dancers are pulling and pulling. I could hear them saying to each other, 'OK, we've got to keep pulling it off,' and I tried to help them, but I was stuck in the Velcro. That was definitely embarrassing."

But aside from those few crazy moments, the mall tour was an excellent experience for Britney. And it was an extra special experience for those fans who got an early glimpse of a superstar on the way to the top. Already the buzz was in the air, and the audience members who hummed along to Britney's tunes were carrying the message—this was the girl to watch!

Radio, Radio

Still, Britney had more than her fans to please. She also had to make an impression on the radio executives who decide what gets played on the airwaves. Most DJs thought Britney's single was super—they recognized ". . . Baby One More Time" as an instant hit. Andrew Jaye of WEOW in Key West, Florida, was quoted in *Billboard* magazine as saying, "It's got one of those 'I can't get it out of my head' hooks that makes you want to go out and dance." Clarke Ingram of WPXY in Rochester, New York, agreed, and added, "Even after hundreds of spins, it's unshakable. Our listeners simply can't get enough of it."

What impressed the radio bigwigs—besides the awesome song, of course—was Britney's sweet but sincerely go-get-'em personality. "Britney shook the hand of every radio programmer in the country," said Jack Satter, Jive Records' senior vice president of pop production. "She's a charming performer and she had a great record to sell."

With pop radio stations firmly in her corner, Britney was positioned for success. Now all the radio world needed was a hit single—and one was definitely on its way!

chapter nine

The Song
and the
Video

ritney's first single, "... Baby One More
Time," was released to radio stations on
November 3, 1998, and was immediately
embraced by the industry and the listening
public alike. All the planning, all the hard work,
and all the mall touring had stirred music
lovers' anticipation. By the time the single hit
the airwaves, the world was ready to embrace
Britney's first musical offering and usher it right
up the charts. The song, which so many fans and
fans-to-be had sampled over the Internet, was
taking the world by storm.

The single scored higher on the *Billboard*
music charts than any other song released that
week, including tunes by Alanis Morissette and
Goo Goo Dolls. Top Forty radio stations across
the country rushed to add it to their playlists.

With its hypnotic beat and catchy lyrics,
"... Baby One More Time" immediately
became a fan favorite. No one was immune to
it—before long, everyone was humming it.
"Everyone who hears it loves it," Britney told
Teen Beat magazine. "It's total attitude—I love it
a lot."

Within a month—and right on her
seventeenth birthday—"... Baby One More
Time" slid up the *Billboard* Hot 100 Music
Chart into the number nine position. It also hit
number six on *Soundscan*. "I heard all about this
on my birthday," Britney told *Tiger Beat*
magazine. "So we all went out to a restaurant

and had a big birthday cake—I was so wrapped up in my birthday, I didn't even focus on how well the single was doing."

Soon there was even more reason to celebrate. By the time Christmas 1998 rolled around, ". . . Baby One More Time" had jumped to number four on *Billboard*'s Hot 100 and on *Radio & Records* CHR/Pop Chart. Then, on December 28, Britney was told her single had gone gold—more than 600,000 copies of the single had been sold. (The song eventually sold more than 900,000 copies.) Britney was so excited, she felt she was going to bust. "It's so neat, it's just crazy, isn't it?" she enthused. "I'm so happy and so thankful—but this is crazy!"

Britney went even crazier when she heard the single on the radio for the first time. "I was home, I'd just gotten off an airplane, and I was in the car heading home, when—oh my goodness!—it came on. It was so weird. I started screaming like a big goob."

A Picture's Worth a Thousand Words

Meanwhile, the video for ". . . Baby One More Time" was steamrolling every major video outlet. Shot in Los Angeles with director Nigel Dick (who also directed videos for the Backstreet Boys, Oasis, and Savage Garden), the video shows Brit dolled up in a schoolgirl's uniform, singing and dancing up a storm. According to Nigel, his job was "to bring life, fun, and color to the video." He did all that and a whole lot more.

The video, which was shot at Venice High School (the school that provided the backdrop of Rydell High in the movie *Grease*), was provocative and sexy, but more importantly it was energetic and filled with life. "I wanted something teenagers could relate to," Britney said. "Something like high school." Kim Kaiman, Jive Records' director of marketing, agreed thoroughly. "Kids love this video. It feels real and it's fun."

Both kids and adults respond well to the video—the cool dancing and the hot music make it a favorite with everyone. Soon, girls began to dress in the style of Britney's video costume. They wore short school uniform skirts, pigtails, and pom-poms and they started showing up at all Britney's live appearances.

The video for ". . . Baby One More Time" was quickly added to active rotation on MTV and The Box, becoming an immediate fan favorite. MTV's senior programmer Tom Calderone hit the mark when he told the *New York Post,* "Britney has star power."

That star power was equally apparent to modeling agencies. Shortly after the release of the video, they began calling Britney in droves, urging the fresh-faced teenager to take the leap into a modeling career. Britney soon announced that she had joined forces with fashion designer

Tommy Hilfiger and that she would be featured prominently in his spring fashion campaign. "I'm a Tommy Girl now," Britney told the *Times-Picayune*.

All the attention might have blown away someone less modest and grounded, but Britney remained her usual sweet self—although she did reveal her determination and her very strong career ambitions. "I've been working toward this moment for a long time," she told *Billboard* magazine. "I just want to keep on building and building."

Road Trip

With radio and video airplay, Britney was fast becoming a major recognizable face in the music field. The media helped, putting Britney's signature smile in every national magazine. Publications like *16, Teen Beat, Tiger Beat,* and *SuperTeen* (which had recognized Britney's appeal early on) started the wave, and it wasn't long before *Teen People, YM,* and *Seventeen* followed suit. Then came the heavy hitters—*Entertainment Weekly, USA Today,* and newspapers in major cities across the country ran huge articles on the gal from Kentwood. Suddenly the fans really began to take notice. "I'd be at a mall, and people would come up to me and ask, 'Are you Britney Spears?'" she told *All-Stars* magazine. And at an MTV appearance in New York City, the fans went wild—girls dressed up in the school uniform outfit, and guys held up signs that read, "I love you, Britney!" and "Will you go to the prom with me?"

Britney had had some experience with adoring fans on her mall tour, but nothing had prepared her for the insanity and pandemonium that her appearances incited among fans now that her single and video were such huge hits. "It's weird, because the guys in 'N Sync can't go out without a bodyguard—fans would do anything to meet them and to touch them," she told *SuperTeen* magazine. "It's unreal." Now the unreality was hitting Britney as well.

As Britney tells it, fame and fans are amazing things—but some people don't understand that Britney needs her privacy like everyone else. "I was at home, and this guy came up to my house," Britney recalled. "I didn't know who he was, and he kept asking people, 'Is Britney home?' It freaked me out so much, I slept with my mama that night! We had to get our phone number changed because so many creepy people like him were calling. And this guy, he knew who my neighbors were—that was just freaky!"

Luckily, most of Britney's experiences with fans have been totally cool. "With me, it's a friend thing," she explains. "Most fans are able to just come up to me and start talking about whatever is on their minds. And that's just fine with me."

'N the Groove with 'N Sync

While the attention from fans was flattering, Britney longed to get back in front of an audience, to recapture the energy and feel the rush of performing. It seemed that a major tour across the country was definitely in order.

Enter 'N Sync. The awesomely popular boy group, which had taken America by storm with their smash hit singles "Tearin' Up My Heart" and "I Want You Back," were touring the country during the fall of 1998. Britney was quickly signed on as the opening act—a role she took on with some trepidation. "It's not easy being an opening act for these guys," she told *Billboard* magazine. "There are all these girls in the audience, and they're all there to see 'N Sync. But ultimately I'm able to win them over. I have guy dancers, and believe me, that helps."

Britney knew about opening acts from her own experience as an audience member. "I've been to see the Backstreet Boys in concert," Britney explained to *SuperTeen* magazine. "And that crowd is there to see the Backstreet Boys, and they're chanting for them. I thought, 'Oh no, I'm gonna die if I get up there and that happens to me!' But luckily, the timing was good for me because everyone knew '. . . Baby One More Time' from the radio. So I was able to look out and see people singing along—it was really cool!"

Of course, the tour also reunited Britney

with her former *Mickey Mouse Club* friends Justin Timberlake and J.C. Chasez, who'd found the monumental success they'd always dreamed of. Britney was psyched to be traveling with friends, and she felt their *MMC* connection broke the ice and made her feel more comfortable with 'N Syncers Lance Bass, Chris Kirkpatrick, and Joey Fatone.

It took Britney only a few days to get accustomed to the mind-bending (and backbreaking) schedule of a national tour. "The first week was really weird," she told *Teen Beat* magazine. "You have to get adjusted to being on a bus and not getting much sleep. But once I got used to it, I loved it. I love being on the road."

Fans flocked to the concerts, and although many may have been there only to swoon over 'N Sync, most were totally in Britney's corner, singing along with her when she belted out ". . . Baby One More Time." "The timing was good, and the song was still doing well on the radio," Britney explained to *All-Stars* magazine. "It was the best feeling, to look out into the audience and see them singing along with me."

On the Road Romance?

While Britney was on the road with 'N Sync, a curious rumor sprang up that she and Justin were a romantic item. Despite Britney's protests to the contrary, the rumor continued to grow and spread. "Girls sometimes send me letters saying, 'Stay away from my man Justin,'" Britney revealed to *16* magazine. "And I'm like, no problem. The guys in 'N Sync are just like big brothers to me. They're very sweet and supportive, but we're really just friends."

But it soon became clear that Britney and Justin were more than just friends. The tabloid newspaper *The Star* reported that the pair were indeed involved in a romance. "I can't believe I'm in the tabloids!" Britney joked when asked about the article—but she did not deny that she and Justin were an item!

Only time will tell if this teenage love connection will continue, but for now, with both Britney and Justin concentrating on their careers, you can be sure it's more often than not a long-distance romance. More than anything, Britney sees Justin as a true friend she can share her experiences with. "The most important thing in any relationship is truth and honesty, and to be able to talk about your feelings," she told *Teen Beat.* "The jealousy thing—that can be a problem. In this business, your friends and boyfriends have to understand how hard you work every day. It isn't all fun and games." Obviously Justin knows a thing or two about that!

Workin' It on the Road

The tour solidified Britney's position as pop princess among her fans. It also helped her develop her performance skills and sharpened her ability to think on her feet. "One time I was on stage and there was a cupcake on the stage, and I was dancing and getting all into it, and I stepped on the cupcake and slipped and fell," Britney told America Online. "There I was, sitting on my butt in the middle of the stage! I had to pretend everything was fine, that it was all a part of the act."

With her four dancers—T.J., Andre, Carissa, and Tonya—Britney and her choreographer, Fatima (who does all the choreography for the Backstreet Boys), were able to create a visually appealing stage show filled with energy and spirit. Britney's dance background made learning the steps a little easier. "In the beginning I was so nervous," she remembers. "But once you start doing it, it becomes second nature, and all that nervous energy helps keep you pumped and moving on stage."

And each night before Britney took to the stage, she had a preshow ritual that kept her grounded and focused. "We all of us get into a circle and say a prayer before each show," she told *Teen Beat* magazine. "God is very important in my life. It's bad because, with all the touring, I don't get to go to church. But I have my prayer book every night, and on the road I always say my prayer before every performance." Britney's faith is of major importance to her. She always wears a band around her wrist engraved W.W.J.D.?—"What would Jesus do?"

Life on the Bus

Hitting the road and touring the country means spending long hours in a tour bus—but bubbly Britney quickly came to think of her tour bus as a second home. "Me and all my dancers ride the bus together, and we act like total goobs," says Britney. "We watch so many movies and we goof around so much."

But as Britney says, it isn't all fun and games. She was pensive when she told *Teen Machine* magazine, "Sometimes I can't sleep, or we get in really late and there's an interview the next morning at six. The worst part of this lifestyle is definitely not getting enough sleep."

... Tomorrow the World

The Britney juggernaut shows no sign of slowing down any time soon. In fact, it looks as if the pace will intensify, with Brit taking her live show to Canada, Germany, France, England, and Germany. And this time, Britney will be the headlining, rather than the opening act.

To help her create an awesome live concert, Britney brought in Johnny Wright, who's currently managing 'N Sync. "I saw her perform, and I was so impressed with her," Johnny told *Entertainment Weekly*. "I'm going to be involved with all her touring and all her live performances. She's basically got all the ideas, I'm just there to help her."

Britney was delighted that Johnny—who's

had tons of experience working with pop performers, including the legendary New Kids On The Block—was on her team. "He'd worked so hard with 'N Sync, and you can tell from the shows they put on what a great job he does," Britney told *16* magazine. "Johnny knows what the audience wants to see."

Working with Johnny means that Britney will be returning to Orlando to live for a while—Orlando, Florida, is Johnny's home base. "I'll have to start rehearsing soon for my tour," she told *Teen Beat.* "I'll live in an apartment or a hotel for a few months—but I definitely need to be in Orlando more because I'll be working directly with Johnny."

With all those hands to help her, there's no doubt Britney is completely ready to tackle any new frontier.

chapter ten

Let's Hear It One More Time!

Britney's debut album, . . . *Baby One More Time*, was released to radio stations and record stores on January 13, 1999, and fueled by the high energy and enthusiasm of the first single, the album soared to number one on the *Billboard* charts. Britney's army of fans had their say in a big way. They guaranteed that the success of her CD would be phenomenal.

The album remained at number one for only a week, then dropped, but within four weeks it was back at number one, smashing the nearest competition (*The Miseducation of Lauryn Hill*) by a whopping 70,000 units. With momentum like that, it wasn't long before Britney's monster hit album was selling double and triple platinum.

And the critics, for once, seemed to agree with the opinion of the fans. *Billboard* magazine called Britney's debut, "a Top 40–ready workout filled with hook-laden songs." They described Brit as a girl who'd been "blessed with a sweet voice," and said her music had "hit a nerve among a teen fan base." Finally, they deemed her "a talent to watch."

According to *Entertainment Weekly,* "this seventeen-year-old ex-Disney princess sounds so soulful and Whitney Houston–assured, it's downright scary."

And the national newspaper *USA Today* raved, "Britney is the first star of 1999's new teen-star crop, and she brings a fresh-faced, girl-next-door appeal."

Of course Britney's fans, who had been rooting for her since the release of the single ". . . Baby One More Time," already knew that Britney had it going on musically. And those same fans couldn't wait to plunk down their money to bring home Britney's CD and share her fun, energetic, "soda-pop" world. As Britney herself told *SuperTeen* magazine, "A lot of the songs deal with love and relationships, but there's one song called 'Soda Pop' which is just a happy, party song."

Since Britney is still a young artist, and since this is her first CD, she didn't have the opportunity to write any of the songs (many artists record songs chosen by their album's producer). But she definitely let her voice be heard when the songs were chosen. "I like a song you can listen to, and it changes," she told *Teen Beat*. "I like songs that you can listen to over and over again, and it always sounds a little different."

In the future, Britney will have an opportunity to write her own songs—something she's already begun doing, and doing well. Her first song, "I'm So Curious," appears on the B-side of her single "Sometimes," and Britney could not be happier about that. "When I first got signed to the record label, there were producers left and right, bringing me songs,"

Britney told *16*. "But all along, I was writing on my own, and 'I'm So Curious' was the first one I showed everyone." Britney also explained how the idea for "I'm So Curious" came to her. "It's all about a girl and a guy, and he likes her and she likes him, but she doesn't know if she should go for it and ask him out. So she says, 'I'm so curious'—like about how this is all going to turn out."

Whether she's writing the songs or singing them, one thing is totally clear—with her debut CD, Britney was able to achieve one of her most cherished musical goals. "I hope my album will make people happy," she told *16*. "I hope that when people hear my music on the radio, it'll make their day a little brighter."

. . . Baby One More Time Makes the Grade!

The tracks on Britney's album touch on universal themes and ideas that everyone can relate to: love, boyfriends, dating, broken hearts, and bouncing back after taking a fall. But Britney also knows that girls just want to have fun, and many of the songs are a salute to good times, friends, dancing, and just plain partying.

Here's the "inside track" on . . . *Baby One More Time*—and our "making the grade" reviews of each totally toe-tapping tune.

● ●

TRACK 1: "...BABY ONE MORE TIME"

Written By: Max Martin

Produced By: Max Martin and Rami in Stockholm, Sweden

Tempo: Definitely up-tempo, a dance tune to the max.

What's It All About: A girl who hopes to get back together with the guy who left her.

What Brit Says: "This song has a lot of attitude. It's got a great beat, and everyone who hears it, loves it."

Grade: A+++ A totally danceable tune with surprisingly moving lyrics. And a catchy chorus definitely doesn't hurt.

● ●

TRACK 2: "(YOU DRIVE ME) CRAZY"

Written By: Jorgen Elofsson

Produced By: Per Magnusson, David Kreuger, and Max Martin in Stockholm, Sweden

Tempo: Mid-tempo, a fun song to tap your foot to.

What's It All About: A girl who's so psyched about her boyfriend, she stays up all night thinking about him.

What Brit Says: "I think everyone knows what the girl in the song is feeling. She just can't stop thinking about, talking about, and dreaming about her boyfriend. She's gone a little 'crazy' in a way, but in a good way."

Grade: A This is a total dance song with lyrics that everyone can truly identify with.

• • • • • • • • • • • • • • • • • • • •

TRACK 3: "SOMETIMES"
Written By: Jorgen Elofsson
Produced By: Per Magnusson and David Kreuger in Stockholm, Sweden
Tempo: Power ballad, with emotion to spare.
What's It All About: A young lady reveals her "sometimes" hidden side to the boy she loves, and lets him know that eventually he'll learn all there is to know about her.
What Brit Says: "I'm really glad they decided to release this song as a single. It's very special and I think everyone will really take something from it."
Grade: A+++ This song, which is the second single release from the CD, is a sweet, gentle love song that'll also keep your head bopping in time to the music. The beat may keep you moving, but the heartfelt lyrics will really touch your heart.

• • • • • • • • • • • • • • • • • • • •

TRACK 4: "SODA POP"
Written By: Mikey Bassie and Eric Foster White
Produced By: Eric Foster White in New York City, NY
Tempo: Up-tempo, a soda pop bottle full of fun and giggles.

What's It All About: Who knows? It's just a whole lotta fun.

What Brit Says: "Sometimes I forget how much I love this song, because it was the first one I recorded. I just think it's the coolest."

Grade: A+ This reggae-inspired track is guaranteed to get you out on the dance floor. We defy anyone to resist its catchy hook and pounding drumbeat.

• • • • • • • • • • • • • • • • • • • •

TRACK 5: "BORN TO MAKE YOU HAPPY"

Written By: Kristian Lundin and Andreas Carlsson

Produced By: Kristian Lundin in Stockholm, Sweden

Tempo: Mid-tempo, a swingy song you can dance to.

What's It All About: A broken romance leaves our heroine pondering life without the object of her affection. She eventually realizes she needs to move away from "a dream of you and me."

What Brit Says: "I like the message of this song. It lets people know it's possible to move on, no matter what."

Grade: A+ The music of a mesmerizing keyboard draws you into the world of lost love and loneliness. Its plaintive chorus should inspire the weepies in anyone with an unfulfilled crush.

• • • • • • • • • • • • • • • • • • • •

TRACK 6: "FROM THE BOTTOM OF MY BROKEN HEART"

Written By: Eric Foster White

Produced By: Eric Foster White in New York City, NY

Tempo: Power ballad deluxe.

What's It All About: A serious tearjerker, this is another song about a love that's been left behind. The girl in the song is begging her beloved to rekindle the fire between them, telling him that he is her "first love" and "true love." Whether he agrees or not is yet to be seen.

What Brit Says: "There's something about a sad love song that really gets to me."

Grade: A++++ The highest grade possible. This song elegantly blends Brit's powerhouse vocals with a lyric that's bound to break your heart. It's a perfect showcase for her awesome talent, a ballad that will bring a tear to the eye of anyone who's ever been in love.

• • • • • • • • • • • • • • • • • • • •

TRACK 7: "I WILL BE THERE"

Written By: Max Martin and Andreas Carlsson

Produced By: Max Martin and Rami in Stockholm, Sweden

Tempo: Slow to mid, a song you and your friends can sway along with.

What's It All About: Britney asserts "I'll Be There" for the one she loves—but the song is also appropriate to sing to a best friend. It's a song of loyalty, trust, and the bonds and strength of friendship.

What Brit Says: "I think this is the best thing you could ever say to a friend."

Grade: A++ So catchy it'll carry you away. (We definitely think this song has the makings of a summer smash!) This is the kind of song you'll want to dance to with your true blue best buds.

• • • • • • • • • • • • • • • • • • •

TRACK 8: "I STILL LOVE YOU"
Written By: Eric Foster White
Produced By: Eric Foster White in New York City, NY
Tempo: Power ballad.
What's It All About: A loving duet with male vocalist Don Philip, this song is a joint declaration of the truest love—both croon, "You are my summer breeze . . . my autumn touch of love . . . my sky, my rain . . ."

What Brit Says: "I really enjoyed singing with Don—I think our voices sound really nice together."

Grade: A+ An anthem of love, this song is destined to become a favorite for couples. This is definitely a perfect "first dance" song, one you'll want to share with someone very special.

• • • • • • • • • • • • • • • • • • •

TRACK 9: "THINKIN' ABOUT YOU"
Written By: Mikey Bassie and Eric Foster White

Produced By: Eric Foster White in New York City, NY

Tempo: Mid-tempo, another swaying song.

What's It All About: We're back in familiar territory, with a lovestruck lady who just can't stop thinking about her boyfriend. But rather than sounding forlorn, our Ms. Britney sounds perfectly content to spend those "days thinkin' about you."

What Britney Says: "I always like singing about relationships, but since I travel so much, I don't have one right now. Still, I know what it's like to spend all day thinking about someone."

Grade: B+ This one's not as intense as "(You Drive Me) Crazy," but it still has enough of that infectious, dancing beat to make it a winner.

• •

TRACK 10: "E-Mail My Heart"

Written By: Eric Foster White

Produced By: Eric Foster White in New York City, NY

Tempo: Mid-tempo, yet easy to dance to.

What's It All About: Something all Nineties ladies can relate to—a girl sends her loving wishes and apologies to a crush who's hit the road. The catch of course—she's sending those messages via E-mail, and she's patiently waiting for him to send one back to her.

What Brit Says: "Anyone with a computer can relate to this one, I think."

Grade: A Looks like true love in cyberspace—Britney's quivery, moving vocals wrap around the lyrics and create a song that's timely in its technology, but timeless in its emotion.

• • • • • • • • • • • • • • • • • • • •

TRACK 11: "THE BEAT GOES ON"
Written By: Sonny Bono
Produced By: Eric Foster White in New York City, NY
Tempo: Up-tempo, funk-a-dellic, and totally retro.
What's It All About: This funky, bouncy tune is a remake of a song that was a smash hit for Sonny and Cher back in the late Sixties—ages ago! It's basically a song that says, "Time passes, so what?"
What Brit Says: "This song was the greatest fun to do. It has a real retro sound I think people will like a lot."
Grade: B Not the best song on the album, but "The Beat Goes On" is a whole lot of hippy, happy fun. The funky background sound effects help a lot, and of course, Britney's voice is right on the money. Throw on those bell-bottoms and turn up the tunes!

chapter eleven

Britney Makes Her Mark

While Britney was recording her album, no one could have predicted the huge success she would have with it. Although everyone who heard it agreed that she had the right stuff—that her voice was strong, clear, and true—a question still remained: Would Britney make it to the very top?

The forecast looked good. Hanson, the Backstreet Boys, 'N Sync, 5, and 98° had opened the door, and pop music had walked right in. On every radio throughout the country and on MTV and VH1, it was pop music that audiences wanted to hear. That audience—the teen audience—had embraced the happy, perky tunes, the sweet love ballads, and the peppy lyrics offered by the boy pop-meisters. Would Britney, as a female, also find a home in the pop music world?

The answer, of course, was a resounding yes! Girl fans, more than ready to embrace a voice of their own, took Britney in and supported her in a big way. GBritney's good looks and sweet, bubbly personality, but they too were listening to the cool tunes. Britney found herself in an incredible position—her single and her album both hit the number one position on the charts simultaneously—a feat not seen since 1992, when kid rappers Kris Kross did it with their debut. "I hoped and dreamed I would have a number one album," Britney told the *New York Post.* "But I never honestly expected it to happen."

Two years before, Britney had been living with her family and friends in a small town in Louisiana. Now she had pulled off an astonishing accomplishment, with the help of teens yearning for her brand of pop music. And you can bet that the media—newspapers, TV and radio stations, and magazines across the country—wanted to talk about it.

National magazines, like *Time* and *Newsweek,* may have thrown compliments Britney's way, but they remained somewhat skeptical about her staying power. *Time,* for example, compared her with eighties pop singer Tiffany—a solo artist whose career slowed down in the U.S. after only one hit. Britney acknowledged the musical comparison but scoffed at the suggestion that her career would be a short one. "We're two totally different people and our sound is totally different," she said.

Newsweek attributed Britney's quick climb up the ladder to the success of the guy groups who came before her, saying she'd "capitalized on two trends at once." *Newsweek* further stated that Britney "has the same cool, sexy style as such bubble-gum groups as the Backstreet Boys. But she's also a teenage girl singing about love in the mold of R&B singers Brandy and Monica."

While some in the media focused on examining Britney's music, others began to take a look at the general pop music phenomenon, which began with the debut of Hanson in 1997. Stan Goman of Tower Records told *USA Today,* "The record companies finally woke up to the fact that they had nothing the teenagers wanted. Now they have some teen stuff out there and it's great."

Of course, every popular movement has its detractors. There were even some people who weren't excited about Britney's music—or the new pop music culture that was so present on the radio. One radio consultant told *USA Today,* "A lot of these records are starting to sound alike. The songs might be testing well, but there's bound to be a backlash eventually." Sean Ross, editor of *Billboard*'s radio magazine, *Airplay Monitor,* was quoted as saying, "Some radio stations have a rule that only one teen act at a time can be in heavy rotation."

If Britney was disillusioned or discouraged by any of the reports, she certainly didn't show it. Truth is, she probably didn't have time to read them. She was way too busy! She appeared as a presenter on the American Music Awards, introducing the Goo Goo Dolls, one of her favorite bands. (She told the *Times-Picayune,* "I love the Goo Goo Dolls, but I was so nervous. All those eyes are on you—and to make it even worse, I was the only one who was out there by myself!") She was also appearing on TV talk shows like *Donny & Marie, The Ricki Lake Show,* and *The Howie Mandel Show*. Everywhere she went, she charmed people with her modesty and her sweetness.

And then, of course, there were the teen magazines, which were all totally delighted to devote endless pages to Britney and her boppin' good-time music. *Teen People* even treated Brit to a fashion makeover, dolling her up in a stunning gown that gave her an ethereal, angelic quality. Britney was floored by the attention. "It's so flattering, all these people doing all this for you," she said.

There are dozens of reasons for the negative views expressed by some critics regarding pop music, but the bottom line is this—the music most beloved by younger fans has *never* been taken seriously! If you do your research, you'll learn that the most important group in modern music history, the Beatles, also faced criticism in their early years. It wasn't until they entered their "experimental" phase that they began to receive unanimous praise. Pop music, with its happy-go-lucky lyrics and boppin' melodies, is often dismissed as "fluff," music without substance, by critics who take pleasure in their own nastiness.

Also, after many years of grunge and alternative music, critics began to equate "good" music with "angry" music. To them, Britney's brand of busting-good-time music seemed totally alien.

But Britney proved them all wrong, and it looks as if her smile-a-minute music is here to stay. With her enthusiasm, energy, sweetness, and talent, Britney's managed to win fans wherever she goes.

Although there will always be pessimistic people determined to tear down popular artists, the fact remains that Britney's music is a hit with her fans. And her warm personality is a hit with everyone.

chapter twelve

The Personal Side of Britney

What's Britney like behind the glitz, the glamour, and the bright lights? It might surprise you to know exactly how much like you she really is!

Britney in Person

Meeting Britney in person is every fan's dream. And everyone who's ever met her reports the same thing—she's absolutely the most down-to-earth, friendly, sweet girl you've ever had the pleasure to know.

Away from the spotlight, Britney is as natural as they come. She speaks with a soft, lilting Louisiana drawl, and her conversation is sprinkled with little Brit-isms, like "Oh my goodness." She constantly calls herself a "goob"—slang for a goofy kid. And she laughs and giggles like crazy.

Britney's all girl, and she loves doing what she calls "girly" things. Number one on that list is shopping—Brit's totally at home at the mall, and she loves spending her time looking through all the latest trendy fashions. She definitely likes trying on new styles—although the clothes she actually buys tend to be comfy rather than fashionable.

Britney also loves experimenting with her makeup and her hair, but when she's done, she quickly washes it all off and ties her locks into a simple ponytail. In fact, being able to look natural is one of the reasons Britney likes New

York City so much. "It's true what they say about New York," she told *Teen Beat*. "No one cares what you look like! If you need to run out and get something to eat, all you have to do is grab a jacket. At home in Kentwood, I would never leave the house unless my hair was just right. But I really like being able to just look natural when I'm not working."

Britney grimaces when she remembers her early makeup experiences—she started wearing makeup when she was fifteen, but she'd been experimenting for years, ever since she'd appeared on the *Mickey Mouse Club*. "When I was fifteen I'd put on that natural glow makeup you buy at the drugstore, and I had my lip gloss," she told *16* magazine. "I thought I was decked out! But now, I look forward to washing it off, not putting it on."

If you met Britney, you might be surprised at how natural she is! "At home, on the road, I never wear makeup, my hair's always tied back, and I'm always in sweats," she told *BOP* magazine. "If a photographer ever got ahold of me, he'd really be surprised!"

Finally, once you got to know Britney, you'd realize that she truly is astonished by all the success she's achieved. She's still the same modest, sweet, unspoiled girl she was before fame and fortune hit hard. "It's weird when people talk to me and act like I'm something so special," she told *16*. "I don't feel any different at all."

Britney at Home

When Britney returns home to Kentwood, she enjoys doing all the normal things she did before fame came calling. These days, she only gets to visit the folks at home every few months or so. The visits are brief but filled with activity.

When she gets home, the first thing she does is plop down on the daybed in her bedroom. "My room is such a girly room," she says. "I collect dolls, so my dolls are everywhere. I have these porcelain collectible dolls, and my *Little Women* dolls are everywhere. I also collect angels. And pictures galore! I have a small room, but it's cute. It's got a blue carpet and a white beanbag chair and a daybed, and of course my stereo and all my CDs. It's the perfect place for me to relax."

After about five minutes of relaxing, Britney's ready to spend some time with the family. Most times they just sit around the dining room table. "I get this major appetite when I get home," Brit admitted to *Tiger Beat* magazine. "My mom cooks baked chicken for me, which is one of my favorites."

Britney also enjoys spending time with her sibs, and when she returns home, hanging with them is the first order of business. "My sister's into sports," she told *SuperStars*. "I did think my sister would be interested in singing—she totally sings like I did when I was younger. But if you tell her to learn a song, she says, 'NO!' Then she picks up a baseball bat. She's a tomboy and she'll tell you exactly what she thinks all the time.

"And my brother, we just talk a lot. He's a great guy. He's a total country boy—he loves football and stuff like that. And he's totally into bodybuilding. He wants to get involved with orthopedics someday—oh yeah, he's a total sports guy!" To prove it, Britney might show you all the awards and trophies displayed on the entertainment center in the living room—that's where her mom and dad keep all the plaques, statues, and cups their brood has brought home.

After hanging with her family, it's time to meet up with her friends, many of whom she's kept since grade school. "We go to the show—the movies, we hang out, we have fun," she told America Online. "When I'm with my friends, I'm totally myself. We never talk about the music business. We mostly talk about them."

After Brit and her friends pack it in, Britney returns home to share girl-talk with her very best friend, her mom. "My mom is someone I can always talk freely to," she told *16* magazine. "There's nothing I can't share with her."

Then it's back to her bedroom, where Brit claims, "I conk out! My favorite way to relax is to take a bath and just go to bed and sleep."

Piggin' Out with Britney

Recently, while filming the video for her second single, "Sometimes," Britney dislocated her knee—while she was kicking up her right leg, her left knee gave out. The video shoot was postponed, and Britney got an unscheduled vacation. Guess what she wanted to do with her time off? "I wanted a good fattening sandwich," she told *Newsweek* magazine. "I went to Jack in the Box and just ate."

So now the truth is out—Britney loves to eat! Her secret is simply this: "I don't overdo anything. I just eat what I want, but I don't go crazy."

Britney also keeps herself in shape with serious exercising. She tries to maintain a fitness regimen on the road, although she admits her current schedule makes that difficult. "When I was recording the album, I used to do fifty sit-ups a night. And I was living in New York City, where you can walk everywhere, and that's great exercise. But with all this traveling, I don't have as much time to exercise. When I'm not doing anything else, I'm sleeping."

The rigors of performing do tend to keep Britney in shape—anyone's who's seen her on stage knows it's quite a workout. "Dancing has always been my favorite way to keep in shape," she told *Teen Machine* magazine. "I love to dance so much. I even try to keep up with classes when I can. There's no better way to stay toned and in shape—and it's so much fun, you forget you're doing something good for yourself."

Lookin' for Love

Like most young girls, Britney dreams about meeting the perfect guy one day. And she's very clear about what qualities constitute the perfect guy. "I'm looking for someone who's cute and funny and sweet, who'll totally support what I do," Britney told *16* magazine. "I want to meet someone who's confident, someone who's happy with themselves. And trust and honesty—those are the two most important things. In friendships and in love, trust and honesty are the foundations."

Britney knows that she might meet that special person anywhere—he might even be a fan! "If I met a person, and I liked that person—I guess he wouldn't be a fan anymore, he'd be a friend," she told America Online.

On the Road Again

The one place Brit is spending most of her time these days is on the road. Traveling the world in a bus or on a plane can make anyone homesick, and Britney is no exception. "I try to remember, the bus is sort of my home-away-from-home," Brit told *Teen Beat*. "But I can't really bring too much on the road. So I always keep my prayer book with me. It goes every-where with me. It reminds me of home and keeps me centered and focused on what's important." That prayer book is never far away. "I always end the day with a prayer," she told *16* magazine. "It helps me sleep better."

When she's traveling, Britney not only stays connected to her faith, she also stays connected to her body and health. In addition to working out whenever she can, she makes sure to take special care of her voice. She sips hot water with lemon or hot tea whenever it feels strained or sore. She also does vocal exercises to keep her voice strong.

Keepin' It Together

Wherever Britney is on any given day, she always remembers how important it is to take care of herself. To that end, you won't find Britney doing anything to hurt her body or her mind—no smoking, drinking, or drugs, ever. "If you don't take care of yourself, you won't have anything," Britney told *SuperTeen*. "Doing stupid things, like taking drugs or drinking—that's only going to mess up everything. I've lived so many of my dreams, why would I ever throw it all away?"

chapter thirteen

Brit Power!

Her Personal Message of Positive Power

One of the things that makes Britney Spears such a special teenager—aside from her awesome talent and rocket-to-the-stars success, of course—is her normalcy. Like you, Britney has spent the past few years growing up and going through the day-to-day trials and tribu-lations of life. Remember, her superstardom is a brand-new thing—she's spent lots of years just being a regular teenager and going through the same things you go through every day.

And even with her monster success, she's still a totally average girl who reacts to life just the way you would. Want a for-instance? How about the fact that she has a major thang for actor Ben Affleck. "He's so cute! And he doesn't have a girlfriend now, does he?" she asked the reporter for *Newsweek* magazine—who was busy doing a story on *her*!

Need another example? How about the time she met the Backstreet Boys for the first time and went positively ga-ga over Kevin Richardson? "He was so beautiful—he's prettier in person!" she told *Teen Beat* magazine. "I was like, oh my goodness, I didn't know what to say. He asked me if we'd met before, in Atlanta, and I was like, 'Oh, sure, of course.' And at that time I'd never even been to Atlanta, so I was a total stupid-head."

Yet Britney can hardly imagine anyone

being starstruck over her—although it happens every day. "Sometimes fans come up to me and totally don't know what to say," she told *16* magazine. "I just talk to them and act completely normal, the same way I'd talk to anyone else. I try to make people feel comfortable because I know how it is. But the funny thing is— whenever anyone comes over and talks to me, it always seems like I look so gooby. I always think—goodness, couldn't you have noticed me when I was looking a little better?"

One of the things Brit is comfortable about is passing along a positive message to her fans. She hopes she can share her experiences with her fans and her friends so they can avoid some of the mistakes and missteps she's made along the road she's traveled.

Of all the experiences Brit has shared with her fans, the one that really tugged at her heart was her last serious relationship. Although she never revealed the guy's name, it was clear she was serious about him when, in June of 1998, she said in an interview, "There's someone special I talk to at home. We have very big phone bills—when I was in Singapore, I made a collect call one night and one call was $150! That's bad—his parents flipped out. It's hard to maintain the relationship, though—we were really serious at one point, but now—I'm going to have to travel so much if I go on tour. So it's kind of sad."

The relationship was one of the most important aspects of Britney's young life. But when she talked about it, she was able to keep it in perspective, and she was happy to share her experiences with her fans. As she told *Teen Machine* magazine, "You fall in love, and suddenly you find yourself with this person twenty-four—seven and it starts getting ridiculous. This person starts telling you what to do and what not to do and you're totally like, 'Oh, you're right!' But then, something just clicked in me one day and I was like, 'What are you doing?'"

Once Britney began actively pursuing her career, she knew she had to make a decision about this particular relationship. Luckily for her, the decision came easily. "He would tell me I'd changed and I'd tell him that he was the one who changed," she told *16* magazine. "He started constantly asking me where I was and what I was doing. I mean, there I was, working like crazy, for hours and hours all day long. I'd come home and call him, and he'd start pressuring me, asking me where I'd been all day. And I was like, 'What do you think? I was working.' He really couldn't understand that you really do get in at four in the morning when you're doing a video shoot. Or that when you're gone all day, you really don't have time to talk on the phone, not even to your mom. All you want to do is go straight to bed. He couldn't understand that, and I couldn't explain it. But I shouldn't have had to explain it. You shouldn't have to apologize for working your butt off. You're like, 'Please leave me alone. . . .' And then you realize, hey, what am I doing? What am I saying? Why am I making excuses for doing the work I love so much?"

Looking back on the experience, Britney realizes that it taught her a serious lesson, which she's glad to share with her female fans—girls who might one day find themselves in similar situations. "I think that no matter how serious a relationship is, you need to be able to have fun and do your own thing," she told *Teen Beat* magazine.

That message—have fun and do your own thing—is one that Brit's taken to heart. Her positive feelings toward herself and her career have given her the strength to be totally true to herself. She gets her strength from her family, her friends, and her faith in God, and she uses her strength to put a positive spin on every aspect of her life.

Fans might look at Britney and think, "Well, she has everything in the world to be positive about, doesn't she? She's famous, beautiful, talented, and she's meeting fabulous people every day. She's also living her dream and doing exactly what she wants to do!" But Britney is able to use her positive thinking power no matter what's going on in her life. And on the days when she's feeling less than wonderful, she always knows she can draw on her inner strength and confidence. "I always try and remember that everything is going to be all right, as long as I stay grounded and remember that I'm surrounded by love. My family, my friends, and now my fans give me so much strength," she told *All-Stars* magazine.

Britney's also a very strong believer in Girl Power (you remember, the kind the Spice Girls used to talk about!), and she translates that power into the simple advice she passes along to fans every day—fans who dream of one day becoming a singer just like Britney. "You've got to work hard and believe in yourself," Britney told America Online. "For me, it's such a great feeling, knowing that people have bought my album and like what I'm doing. But it's also important for people to like what they're doing. It's important to enjoy every minute of life. Whether it's singing you love, or sports or writing or whatever. You've just got to have faith in yourself, and believe you can do it."

Without Peers

Like most teenagers, Britney is well aware of the problem of peer pressure. She knows that teens face a lot of it, and she herself has had to deal with it from time to time. But Britney also knows that at the end of the day, the last person you see in the mirror is you, and she would never want to do anything to jeopardize her future. That means she stays true to herself. "I know it's hard, when your friends are telling you to try this or that," Britney told *SuperStars* magazine. "But it's very important for each individual to decide what's important to them, and then for each person to live their life based on that decision. I know that I always have to be true to myself, so when something comes up, and it's not right for me, I know it immediately."

Down But Not Out

Sometimes life throws a curve ball to even the brightest superstar. While filming the video for her second single, "Sometimes," Britney had a bad fall and twisted her knee. Although she took some time off to recuperate, staying off her feet to avoid inflicting more injury on the knee, it eventually became clear that she was going to need more help than just a little rest and relaxation could give. When she finally went into Doctors Hospital in New Orleans, Dr. Tim Finney—who's the chief physician for the New Orleans Saints football team—removed a one-inch piece of loose cartilage from her knee.

Britney was a little upset that the full extent of the injury hadn't been discovered right away, but she was pleased that the surgery went well and was determined to get back in dancing shape as soon as possible. She began working daily with a physical therapist who exercised the leg to keep it strong. She also began working out more seriously with hand weights, using them to strengthen her upper body and cardiovascular system. For several weeks, she used a pair of crutches to help her get around. "I get frustrated because when I go to make a public appearance, I can't dance," she told *16* magazine. When she filmed the "Walt Disney Easter Parade Special" in MGM Studios, she needed a golf cart to take her around the park, and when it came time to perform, she had to stay seated on a large chair while she sang "... Baby One More Time" to a crowd of screaming fans.

Britney sent the following message out to her fans, who were so concerned and worried (especially after hearing nasty Internet rumors suggesting that she might never dance again): "I want to thank my wonderful fans and all of the people who have offered their love and support during this time."

As you might have expected, the injury didn't keep her down. Before long she was back on her feet and moving to the beat—one more time!

chapter fourteen

*Special
Fan
Section!*

How to Reach Britney
Snail Mail
Britney Spears Fan Club
P.O. Box 250
Osyka, MS 39657

Britney absolutely loves getting fan mail—
she says she does her best to get to as many
letters as possible. Be sure and include a photo
of yourself—it makes a letter much more
personal. Also, if you include a self-addressed,
stamped envelope, you're more likely to receive
a reply. To really get your letter noticed, use
pretty baby-blue colored stationery. It's her
favorite, so it'll attract her attention. And don't
stress out if you don't get a reply right away—
be patient. You know Britney's schedule is
demanding, and she really doesn't want to
disappoint you.

E-Mail
Britney@peeps.com

Britney checks in with her E-mail as often
as she can, although she admits she gets a little
slack when she's away on tour. E-mail is an easy
way to get connected to Britney.

Britney on the Web

The Internet is absolutely loaded with opportunities to chat with other die-hard Britney
devotees. The official Britney Web sites are:

http://www.peeps.com/Britney
http://www.asylum.com/music

There are dozens of alternative sites to check out as well; here are just a few of the best ones (For easy access to these sites, you'll want to begin with a search engine like Yahoo or Dogpile. Type in the name Britney Spears, and you'll be in the loop):

- wallofsound.go.com/artists/britneyspears/home.html
- reach.to/britney
- www.geocities.com/SunsetStrip/Stadium/7135/
- www.geocities.com/Hollywood/Agency/1951/Britney.html
- listen.to/britney_spears
- www.angelfire.com/hi2/britspears/britney.html
- come.to/britneyspearsaz

Web Pages

There are also over 850 Britney Web Pages out on the Internet. These Web Pages, usually created by fans for fans, are a great way to reach out and chat with Web friends. But be warned: These Web Pages are unofficial, and often include information that is outdated, unsubstantiated, and downright untrue. Log on at your own risk. And definitely don't believe everything you read on the Web!

Britney Online

Britney often drops in at America Online to participate in chats with her fans—check out AOL for info on upcoming Britney events.

You can also post messages to Britney through AOL at keyword: Britney.

BE FOREWARNED! Britney *never* goes into chat rooms on her own! Although she loves participating in Online chats, it's always through America Online. If you're chatting somewhere else, and someone claims to be Britney Spears—don't believe it, 'cause it's not true!

Britney Facts at Your Fingertips

Real Full Name: Britney Jean Spears

Nickname: Brit

Birthday: December 2, 1981

Family: 'Rents are Lynne and Jamie, her big brother, Bryan, is 21, and her sweet sister, Jamie Lyn, is 8.

Pets: She's got a Rottweiler named Cain.

Height: 5'5"

Hair: It's dark blond, but when the light hits it a certain way, it can look almost strawberry blond.

Eyes: Brown

FAVORITES

Music: Mariah Carey, Prince, Aerosmith, Backstreet Boys

Sport: Basketball, swimming, gymnastics

Color: Baby Blue

Food: Pasta, hot dogs, and ice cream (specifically cookie dough flavor)

Hobbies: Shopping, watching movies (especially romantic comedies), and reading trashy romance novels.
Disney Character: Goofy
Walt Disney World Ride: Space Mountain
Cereal: Cocoa Puffs
Signature Saying: Britney often interjects her sentences with "Oh goodness!"
Wears: Tommy Hilfiger

Basic Britney—How You Can Look Like Her!

So, you say you want to capture Britney's unique and totally trendy look. It's not as tough as you might think—here are some basic steps you can take if you want to look just a little bit like Britney.

Hair

Britney likes to wear hers straight and long. She keeps her bangs trimmed so they just brush her eyebrows. The next time you get your hair cut, ask for a style that frames your face. For a night out, Brit might crimp her hair to achieve a wavy, mussed look. And these days, she's also in to wearing extensions, which add supersensational volume to her straight hair. If you can't afford extensions, you can crimp like a pro using a curling iron—all it takes is a little practice and patience, and you can achieve the amazing, full-bodied Britney look you love.

To protect her hair from the sun, Brit likes wearing baseball caps and hats. You should get into that habit as well, especially when the summer sun is really blazing down.

Makeup

No lie—Britney really doesn't like wearing too much of it when she's just hanging out. That could be because she has to slap on so much of it for her stage performances. For your best everyday Britney look, keep it simple:

• Start with a matte foundation that perfectly matches your skin tone. Apply with a sponge to keep the foundation from looking thick. Blend downward, toward your jaw. When the foundation is totally blended into your skin, reach for a light matching power and top the foundation off so it doesn't look wet or shiny.

• Brush a mauve or light pink blush on the apples of your cheeks. Blend the color in to avoid a streaky line. Using a huge blush brush, add touches of color to your temples and jawline—that'll pull it all together beautifully.

• Line your eyes with a simple dark brown pencil. (Use taupe or gray if your eyes are very light.) Speckle the pencil along your lash line to avoid a sharp, harsh line. To get Britney's look, *never* use liquid eyeliner, or colors like dark blue or purple.

- Use a brown-black mascara—one coat will keep the clumps away.
- Brown, mauve, pale purple, and pink—feminine and natural are the adjectives to remember when selecting eye shadow. To achieve Britney's look, brush a neutral shade on your lid, with a lighter, complementary shade on the brow.
- For full, Britney-bright lips, line yours with a pencil. Stay in the pink, peach, and mauve family (never any reds or dark browns!) Fill in with matte lipstick. For a natural everyday look, stick to lip gloss in a fresh, fun flavor.
- Keep your look natural at all times, and stay away from any makeup that leaves you looking shiny or garish. Fresh, clean, and natural is the way Britney likes to look every day.

For Nighttime Sizzle!

When Britney heads out for a night on the town, she adds a little more sparkle to her makeup with—glitter, naturally! And you can get the same look with a minimum of fuss. Apply your regular makeup, then accent with glitter and sparkles—use eye shadows and blush that have glitter blended right in. Nighttime is also the right time for brighter colors, so be sure and use a hotter pink lipstick to really add some pizzazz!

- For an all-over extrasensational look, use body glitter on your shoulders and arms. And don't forget to glitter up your hair a little—all the better to catch the bright night lights!

Clothes

Tommy Hilfiger, Betsey Johnson, Bebe— when Brit's out on the town, she loves dressing up in designer duds. (Britney is one of Tommy Hilfiger's models for Tommy Jeans—you may have already seen her in his ad campaign, along with singers Mya and Q-Tip.)

Out of the limelight, Britney is into comfy, trendy, casual, and cute outfits. She loves miniskirts with little T-shirts; rolled-up jeans and short-sleeve, scoop-neck sweaters; sneakers, sandals, and, of course, her beloved platform shoes. Basically, Britney likes to wear current fashions without getting too way-out. And she likes her clothes to fit properly—you'll never catch her in anything tight, because she loves to be comfortable.

On stage, it's a different story. Under the spotlight, Britney appears in short, midriff-revealing tops, baggy, low-hanging pants, and Skechers. But that's showbiz! When she's performing, Brit needs to be comfortable, but she also wants to catch the eye.

Britney also tends to change her look depending on where she is. When she's at home, she likes to look as natural as possible, but when she's up in New York City working on her music, anything can happen. "Things I would wear in New York I would never wear at home," she told *Teen People* magazine. "People at home would look at you and think you were crazy. In New York, you can walk out with purple hair and it doesn't matter." Not to worry, though—Brit totally bagged the idea of dying her hair purple!

• To get that Britney look: Team up baby Ts (in Britney's favorite color, baby blue) with denim mini-skirts and platform sandals. Or wear a short-sleeved cotton shirt over slick Capri pants. You also might check out those adorable knit tank tops that look so super over faded, wide-legged jeans.

• You don't have to spend a lot to look like Brit! Check out vintage clothing stores for adorable Capri pants, baby Ts, and even platform shoes.

• A Britney Fashion Factoid: Britney loves the way Jennifer Love Hewitt and *Friends* star Jennifer Aniston dress. She calls them her fashion icons.

Jewelry

Again, simplicity is key. Britney loves silver rings and necklaces, and drop earrings. She's also into arts-'n'-craftsy type jewelry—things that look handmade, like beads and Puka shells. She definitely avoids flashy stones, and she's totally *not* into piercing anything other than her earlobes.

Accessories

To pull it all together, Britney loves pulling on a hat—baseball caps, floppy hats, berets, she loves them all. She also loves fashionable belts, kneesocks, and backpacks (she really loves the see-through, balloon styles that are all the rage now). Finally, no Britney 'do would be complete without those adorable clip barrettes—Britney likes the sparkly ones shaped like butterflies. When it comes to accessories, the thing that Brit looks for is fun as well as fashion—she's willing to take a risk and try out something new and funky.

A Britney Must!

Brit loves painting her toenails! Her favorite colors are vampy rusty reds and the palest of pinks. It's a must for all the strappy sandals Britney wears during the summer months!

Doin' the Britney Workout

Take one look at Britney, and you'll know the girl is totally into staying in shape. And she doesn't starve herself either—that's something she knows is completely uncool. "I love to eat," she confesses. "And I love really fattening things. I love Southern food, like fried chicken and barbecue and mashed potatoes—I don't deny myself anything I love!"

So how does she keep herself in prime

baby T condition? Well, as you can imagine, performing every night helps. When you're on stage, under hot lights, dancing up a storm, it's easy to sweat off a few pounds! "It's a complete workout, believe me," Brit told *16* magazine. "You're constantly moving, sweating, and dancing—it is strenuous beyond belief."

But in addition to her on-stage athletics, Britney believes in maintaining a healthy exercise program—and you can, too! Just turn on your Britney CD and let the music move you. It's time to get those muscles toned and that heart pumping!

Step One—Warm It Up!

Brit knows it's important to never ever rush into exercising. Without stretching out your muscles, you're bound to end up with a painful cramp or worse. So do your warm-ups!

1. Stretch and breathe! Take deep breaths and fill your lungs with oxygen. As you breathe, raise your arms up and bring them down.

2. Stretch those legs! Do slow leg lunges to stretch out those muscles in the backs of your legs.

3. Move around! Get that blood pumping! Run lightly in place to loosen yourself up. Or better still, dance around like crazy. As Britney says, dancing vigorously is an excellent way to exercise. It'll really get that heart rate up!

The Workout

Sit-Ups

They're yucky, but Britney swears by them. One hundred of them every night! Be sure and practice proper posture so you don't hurt your back. Here's how:

• **Lie on the floor.** Place your hands on the sides of your neck, lightly. Spread your legs shoulder-width apart and bend your knees.

• **Sit up slowly.** Let your abdomen, not your back or neck, do the lifting.

• **Crunch it.** Bring your torso up off the floor, but don't sit all the way up. Just that slight movement will give you that "crunch" you're looking for.

• **Bring it on down.** Return to your original position slowly, with no jerking motions. Keep your movements fluid.

Leg-Lifts

• **Lie on your side.** Use your arms to keep yourself upright. Extend your legs and point your toes.

• **Lift.** Raise your leg slowly to a count of eight, until it is pointing toward the ceiling.

• **Lower your leg** to a count of eight.

• **Repeat 16 times.** Then flip over and do the other side.

Weights

To keep her arms looking buff and toned, Britney works out with weights. And don't let the concept of weights scare you—they won't turn you into Ms. Arnold Schwartzenegger! Two light (2½-pound) dumbbells are all it takes.

• When you're out doing your power walk, carry one dumbbell in each hand. It makes your workout even more powerful.

• Lift 'em! Hold the weights in your hands and bend your elbows. Lift one arm to the sky eight times, then lift the other eight times. Do three repetitions of this exercise.

Walk It!

Walking is much better—for you and your knees!—than jogging or running. Grab your Walkman, pop in a Britney tape, head to the park, and just walk. Keep a good pace—this isn't strolling time—but don't kick it up a notch to a jog. Listen to ". . . Baby One More Time" and just walk to the beat.

Staying Active

One of the best ways Britney knows to stay in shape is to stay active—to do the things you love to do anyway! Want some examples? How about biking, swimming, roller blading, hiking, playing basketball—or any other sport—with your friends! All these activities help you burn calories while you're having fun. And if you can get a great big group of your best buddies to join you, you'll have a most excellent time!

One of Britney's favorite activities is swimming—it's a great way to tone up your muscles and keep your heart strong. But the key to staying active is to choose something you're really into. That way you'll do it every day.

Another activity Britney can't do without is in-line skating. She loves lacing up the skates and taking a spin around the park. Of course, she never forgets to gear up, and neither should you—always remember to strap on the wrist, elbow, and knee guards, and pull on a helmet.

Keep It Cool—Down!

No matter what kind of workout you've chosen, be sure to cool down after you're done. Cooling down simply means giving your body a chance to relax. Doing some deep breathing and some bending and stretching exercises will give your body a chance to cool down properly.

Some "Britney Workout" Tips

1. Don't overdo it! Exercise is supposed to make you feel great, not rotten. If you push yourself too hard, you're bound to end up with seriously sore muscles.

2. Don't get freaky about it! If you start obsessing about your workout, or if it starts becoming too much "work" and not enough

fun, it's time to cut down. Remember, if you enjoy what you're doing, you'll do it more often—and reap the healthy benefits.

3. Drink lots of water! Before, during, and after your workout, you'll need to replace the water you've sweated out of your body. Keep pouring the water in, and you'll get most excellent results out of your body. In fact, it's a good idea to drink tons of water each day no matter what you're doing. It'll make your skin look great and keep you feeling fine.

4. Do exercise when you're feeling blue. The burst of energy will make you feel better.

5. Do exercise to music—Britney's music will do very nicely!

Party On—Throw a Britney Bash with Your Friends!

Looking for a new, totally funky, and unique idea for your next best-buddy get-together? How about a Britney Bash? Here's how:

• Invite your favorite Britney-fan friends for a festive sleepover—your best friend, your cousin, the girl in science class—anyone who shares your love of Britney and her good-time music.

• Choose Brit's favorite tunes! To get your party in gear, crank up the music—and make it music Britney herself would completely get into. To get the room dancing, slide in a Backstreet Boys or Robyn CD; to mellow out, switch to Mariah Carey; to pick up the energy level, listen to Prince's *Purple Rain* soundtrack CD. And of course, keep ... *Baby One More Time* close to the CD player, and have a Britney sing-along whenever the mood strikes you.

• OK, now it's time to eat! If Britney was at your house, she'd tell you to throw some hot dogs on the grill and stock up on the cookie dough ice cream. And make sure to keep some healthy snack foods around—things like veggies and dip and fruit slices. Nothing too fancy—Britney likes basic, good-tasting food best.

• Girls just gotta have fun, and that's what you're going to want to do at your girly gala. What would Britney like to do with you and your friends? Well, you could rent a slew of movies, like *My Best Friend's Wedding, The Horse Whisperer, Titanic* (OK, so it's going to be a long night—make lots of popcorn), and *Steel Magnolias,* and laugh, cry, and snack out all night. Or you could crank up the tunes and dance till you drop. Another very cool idea—experiment with makeup and new hairstyles. You can try new colors on one another, or give your best friend that 'do you've been dying to try. Try out body glitter, temporary tattoos—anything that looks cool and new to you.

• Talk about guys! Just like you, Britney adores indulging in girltalk, especially about cute guys. She definitely wouldn't mind joining you in an all-night discussion about which

Backstreet Boy is the cutest. (She'll tell you she went totally loopy over Kevin, who she says is absolutely gorgeous in person.)

• Conk out and sleep. After all that activity, you'll certainly be ready for bed.

chapter fifteen

Pop Quiz

Could You and Brit Be Best Friends?

You're crazy about Britney's brand of pop music. You think she's one of the coolest singers you've ever heard. And of course, you can't get enough of her awesome album and her totally watchable videos.

But do you have what it takes to be Britney's absolute best friend? Do you share tastes in music, movies, and hobbies? What about values, ideals, and ambitions—think both you and Brit are in agreement? Well, there's only one way to find out—read this book, then take this little quiz and see if you've got what it takes to spend quality best-buddy time with Britney Spears.

1. You and Britney are getting ready to spend the afternoon together. What activity have you planned?

a) A day at the movies—a romantic comedy or a major five-hankie tearjerker, if possible.

b) Shopping at the local mall—although you might just do a lot of trying on and little actual buying.

c) Hanging out in your room, experimenting with makeup and listening to music.

2. Britney's off on another awesome tour of the U.S. Do you . . .

a) Expect to be invited along—after all, you're her best friend!

b) Get resentful and annoyed—you hate it when she's gone for long periods of time.

c) Smile and tell her you'll be waiting to hear all about it when she gets back.

3. You know Britney is way close with those 'N Sync babes, Justin and J.C. Do you . . .

a) Grill her about the guys—are they dating anyone? Could she fix you up?

b) Constantly ask her to tell you stories from the road.

c) Cut Brit a break—when the two of you hang out, you've got other things to talk about.

4. You're buying Britney some CDs for her birthday. What do you purchase?

a) Mariah Carey, Prince, and that new Backstreet Boys album, as soon as it's available

b) Classical music or operas

c) You don't buy any—you figure she probably has plenty of CDs already.

5. You and Britney are busy studying—what subjects is she tutoring you in?

a) Square dancing

b) History and English

c) Math

6. You've got a brand-new boyfriend—how does that affect your relationship with Britney?

a.) It doesn't—best friends stay best friends, even when a guy comes into the picture!

b) It changes it slightly—you tend to spend most of your "girltalk" time chatting about him rather than the two of you.

c) It totally alters it—after all, you've got to spend all your free time with him, don't you?

7. You want to have a singing career just like Britney's. Do you . . .

a) Constantly ask her to help you get a record deal.

b) Ask her advice occasionally and really listen to what she tells you.

c) Assume Brit wouldn't want you as competition.

8. It's a beautiful afternoon and Britney has the day off. You both decide to . . .

a) Get active—swimming, a goofy game of one-on-one basketball, or a long walk in the park.

b) Get silly—go for a ride with the car top down, singing along to the radio.

c) Get lazy—pull out the lawn chairs and the sunglasses, mix up a pitcher of iced tea and lounge out.

9. Which song on ...*Baby One More Time* is Britney's favorite?

   a) "The Beat Goes On"

   b) "...Baby One More Time"

   c) "Soda Pop"

10. Your friends at school are gossiping about Britney and they urge you to tell them your secrets. You . . .

   a) Reluctantly join in, telling a few stories and revealing a few confidences.

   b) Tell them no, your friendship with her means too much.

   c) Babble about everything the two of you did last weekend.

Answers

1. Trick question—all three activities would make Britney smile.

2. C. Traveling and touring are major parts of Brit's career—she'd want your support.

3. C. Are you her friend 'cause you like *her* or the 'N Sync guys?

4. A.

5. B.

6. A. Britney knows that friendships last forever, and she'd want to know you felt the same way, even if a new guy did enter the picture.

7. B. Brit's glad to answer your questions—just don't ask 'em every other minute!

8. Another trick question—any of the three would be excellent!

9. C. Brit's admitted to having a soft spot for "Soda Pop."

10. B. Loyalty is important to Britney, and she'd want to know she could trust you.

HOW'D YOU DO?

10 Matches: Total Girl Power!—You and Britney would definitely be buds forever.

7–9 Matches: Not Too Bad—You know a lot about Brit, and would probably get along famously with her.

4–6 Matches: Yikes! You and Brit don't have much in common besides great taste in music.

0–5 Matches: No way! Better read this book "one more time," 'cause what you don't know about Britney would fill a book of your own!

chapter sixteen

Britney's
Ultrabright
Future

With her talent, determination, and will to succeed, Britney Spears's star is destined to shine brightly for years to come. The only question is, will that star be shining in the music business or in movies and TV?

Although she's found fame as a pop singer extraordinaire, Britney's also been dabbling in acting, something she's been interested in since her early days in New York City, when she made her debut on the Off-Broadway stage in *Ruthless.*

In 1999, Britney appears in three episodes of the WB network's smash hit show *Dawson's Creek,* where she will help create a character for herself—a character that may eventually spin off into a TV show of her own! Although Britney's tour schedule is demanding—and sometimes overwhelming—she's working closely with Columbia Tri-Star Television, the studio that developed *Dawson's Creek* and *Party of Five.* Her entertainment lawyer, Larry Rudolph, told the *New York Post,* "Britney is developing a relationship with the top TV company for the type of series she might want to do." That means Britney might be ruling the TV airwaves very soon!

And although Britney's always remained focused on her music career, she's never been shy about reflecting on her future—a future that just might include acting. "I would definitely like to get into films," she told America Online.

"That would be fun! I've already done regional commercials and theater, so I have some experience. It would be an exciting thing, wouldn't it?"

It makes sense that Britney might want to explore other outlets for her abundant talents. After all, she's been quoted as admiring Madonna, who's known for her chameleon qualities—reinventing herself from pop icon to movie star whenever a good film role comes along. And Britney's voice has already been compared to Madonna's—a comparison Britney considers a great compliment. "I like being compared to Madonna, because I totally respect and admire her," says Britney. "She's grown so much as an artist, and she's always changing. I think she's an amazing artist." And she told *USA Today,* "I'd love to do a duet with Madonna 'cause she's just, like really out there. I think it would be a real shocker to everyone if we performed together."

There's no reason Britney couldn't become an equally amazing artist. And there's also no reason Britney won't eventually shock the world with her own awesome abilities. Everyone who comes into contact with her recognizes that she has something very special to offer the world. Jeff Fenster from Jive Records told *Billboard* magazine that Britney was "intriguing" and that her talent was "boundless." Nigel Dick, the director of her video, praised her ability in front of the cameras. And Barry Weiss of Jive Records told *USA Today* that Britney has "a real girl-next-door appeal. Every girl wants to be like her and every guy wants to get to know her."

But singing and acting aren't the only things in Brit's future. This bright young lady totally recognizes the importance of education, and she's looking forward to working out with her brainpower one day soon. "I do want to go to college," she told America Online. "Right now I'm focusing on my career, of course, but I definitely want something to fall back on. This business is crazy—you never know what's going to happen from day to day." There's no doubt that Britney will get her degree one day, perhaps majoring in her academic love, English. "There's so much I want to do in my life," she says. "I've got my whole life ahead of me, and I think if I put my mind to it, I can do anything!"

What the Stars Say about the Star!

If you ask Britney, she'll tell you that the future probably hinges more on hard work than horoscopes, but she's definitely one to keep an eye on the star signs. And according to Britney's charts, the future's so bright she's gonna have to wear serious shades!

Like many Sagittarians, Britney has diverse talents. The music, theater, and movie worlds are filled with stars born under this illustrious sign, like Brad Pitt, Katie Holmes, Kim Basinger, and Brendan Fraser. Blessed with candor and honesty, those born under the sign of the Archer tend to be straightforward and truthful, with a need to reach out and touch others. That could be why Britney is so inspired to touch fans with her music.

Britney also has the cheerfulness and friendliness often attributed to Sagittarians. That means that when the chips are down, she's got the positive and upbeat attitude it takes to keep forging ahead. There's no doubt she'd be able to move smoothly into the acting biz, but if things didn't go her way in the beginning, she'd still be able to keep a smile on her face anyway.

Acting often beckons to those born between November 23 and December 21. Sagitarrians enjoy studying human nature, and they often have a good time playing different roles with their friends.

And finally, those born under this sign often say they feel lucky. Certainly Brit will tell you she feels lucky to be doing what she's doing. But the truth is, luck has little to do with it. Those born under this sign enjoy taking chances and plunging into new things with a lot of energy and enthusiasm. That's probably got more to do with Britney's success than something as hard to define as luck. The truth is that Britney's optimism and happy-go-lucky attitude, mixed liberally with her ambition and willingness to work hard, have combined to bring her to this point in her career.

And that means that whatever Britney wants to accomplish, she probably will!

Crowing for Britney!

In Chinese astrology, Britney was born (1981) in the year of the Rooster! This ancient mystic study, which dates back to the Ming Dynasty (which ruled China 350 years ago) holds that people take on the characteristics of the animal that governs their year of birth.

So what traits might Britney share with a rooster? Her singing calls up sunshine. Plus, people born under the sign of the Rooster tend to be very honest and straightforward—two qualities Britney definitely exhibits.

Rooster-year chicks also tend to be multi-talented and enthusiastic—certainly two more traits you could use to describe Brit. They do well in music and the arts because they really love to work hard at their craft.

Those born under the Rooster sign make excellent best friends because they are so loyal and devoted—if you want to share a secret with someone who absolutely won't tell, share it with a Rooster person! They also love to entertain and make people smile—two things Britney does every day!

What does the future hold for Britney using this method of astrology? Well, 1999 is the year of the Rabbit, and according to Chinese astrology, this year holds tons of positive changes for Roosters. It looks as if Britney's headed for more success, as well as big changes in her career (Hmm, could that acting gig on *Dawson's Creek* really be leading to big things? Looks like it, according to this chart). Keep your eye on Britney—1999 might just be her biggest year yet!

Romance, Romance

Britney's definitely a romantic at heart— you can hear it in her voice when she croons love songs like "Born to Make You Happy" and "I Will Still Love You." But her experiences have taught her to be careful when it comes to love and never to settle for someone who isn't absolutely right for her.

Britney wouldn't mind dating someone who worked in show business, and she certainly wouldn't refuse a date with someone tall, dark, and gorgeous. But she's learned that the most important things in a relationship are trust and understanding, and that a beautiful heart and soul are what really makes a guy a winner. So while she will always keep her eyes open for Prince Charming, she's not going to waste her time kissing any toads.

Right now, Britney's career is the most important thing to her. But she's keeping an open mind and an open heart, and she knows someday she'll find a guy who's perfect for her.

The Final Word

Whatever Britney does in her life, there's no way she'll completely give up her first love, music. After all the years she's spent working to get to the top, you can bet she'll never stray far from the one thing that makes her most happy. "I always knew this was what I wanted to do," she has said. "It's been a lot of work, but it's been absolutely worth it!"

Britney 2000: To the Millennium and Beyond!

Britney Spears has reached a level of success most singers can only dream about—and she's only eighteen years old! And if 1999 was successful, you can just bet the year 2000 and beyond will be bright and blazing for this incredible young superstar.

Diamonds Are a Girl's Best Friend!

There's no doubt that the year 1999 will always be memorable to Britney. It was a year that brought her tons of success, buckets of awards, and countless number one singles. And what does Britney have to say about it all? How about her signature phrase, "Oh my goodness!"

By the end of 1999, Britney's monster hit album, ". . . Baby One More Time," had spent more than 48 weeks on the Billboard 200 charts—in the top ten, no less—and the album had been certified Diamond, which means more than 10 million CDs have been sold! "I never could have imagined anything like this," Britney told *SuperTeen* magazine. "I had hoped the album would do well—but this is just amazing. I remember, last year I was excited because my single went gold—I was like, 'YAY!' All this hard work has paid off, and I'm really blessed."

In fact, Britney's debut album was second in 1999 only to the Backstreet Boys' *Millennium*. "I can't even think about that!" she excitedly told *Tiger Beat* magazine. "They're sooo great!"

Crazy About Britney!

The success of Britney's first two singles, ". . . Baby One More Time" and "Sometimes," was topped by her third, "Drive Me Crazy." The song, a danceable up-tempo tune about a love so strong it "drives you crazy," was chosen to be on the soundtrack of the movie of the same name—*Drive Me Crazy,* a romantic comedy starring Melissa Joan Hart, of *Sabrina the Teenage Witch* fame. (Bet you didn't know the movie was originally titled *Next To You!* The producers of the movie took notice of how popular Miss Brit had become, and changed the name of the whole movie to focus on Britney's awesome song.) To return the favor, Melissa appeared in Britney's "Drive Me Crazy" video—a video that spent tons of time on MTV's *Total Request Live.* In it, Britney starts off as a plain-Jane waitress, with glasses and a frilly pink waitress uniform. She transforms herself into a golden-maned goddess in an emerald green tube top and skin-tight black vinyl pants. Melissa appears as a fellow diner employee— one who serves up the ice cream records for the DJ. "Melissa is like, the coolest girl," Britney told *16* magazine. "I was a little nervous about meeting her, because she's such a big star. But she's so professional, and just so wonderful."

Melissa returned the compliment, and more, in *Teen Beat* magazine when she said, "Britney is a great girl and a good friend. She's so sincere and genuine. The only thing is, she gets so tired. She works so hard, and she gets really tired out. I don't think anyone realizes what a hard worker she is." Melissa and Britney are definitely both hard workers—one of the things they discussed on the video set was the possibility that Britney might do a guest appearance on *Sabrina* (after all, the pop group 'N Sync made just such an appearance last year—to rave reviews!).

Miss Brit agreed to appear on the show, and it aired in November 1999. On the episode, Sabrina "blips" Britney into her room, and learns a little bit about the Britney lifestyle (along with some cool new dance steps from the Brit-meister). At the end of the show, Sabrina "blips" Britney back onto the stage so she can perform her concert show—a show Sabrina and her friend Harvey attend together. Although Britney has no memory of her magical trip through time and space, she does recognize her friend Sabrina—and shares a little wave with her from the edge of the stage. "I really liked working with Britney," Melissa told *16* magazine. "She's a lot of fun to hang around with, and she's a great worker. We got along great, and now we're really good friends."

When the film *Drive Me Crazy* was released to theaters in October 1999, Britney and Melissa both traveled the country, doing publicity to promote the movie—and by the reception she received, you would have thought Brit was the star of the movie. "Everyone's been so nice to me," Britney told *All-Stars* magazine. "Wherever I go, Melissa and I are treated so well—it's just beautiful, meeting the fans this way."

Bottom's Up!

Britney's fourth single is the delicate ballad "From the Bottom of My Broken Heart." For the video for this single, Britney shuns the usual showbiz glitz and glamour for a really simple look—she wears jeans and a funky hat as she sits on the steps, singing sweetly and sadly about the love that got away. "Sometimes I think people just know me for those upbeat songs, like 'Drive Me Crazy,' Britney told *Bop* magazine. "But I think there's nothing like a real weepy ballad. A song like 'From the Bottom of My Broken Heart' can really make me a weepy girl."

Back on the Road with LFO!

On March 8, 2000, Britney will begin yet another United States tour (with pop trio LFO, the guys who brought you the super hit singles, "Summer Girls" and "Girl on TV"). Of course, the guys couldn't be happier about going on the road with Britney and opening for her—after the success of her last tour, LFO can expect to be opening to huge crowds all across the country. "She's been so successful, it's impressive," LFO's Rich Cronin told *Entertainment Teen* magazine. "We're definitely psyched and honored to be going on the road with her. I know we'll put on a great show for all the fans who come out and see us."

And you better believe Britney's looking forward to being on the road again—although she admits she sometimes gets tired of being away from home so much. "On the one hand, I love touring," she told *SuperTeen* magazine. "But on the other, when I see my bedroom at home, I'm like, 'Oh my goodness, that looks soooo good I just can't believe it. And rehearsing is hard—I have three weeks of rehearsal before the tour."

Britney's proud of her concerts, and she's totally psyched about being involved in every aspect of them. "My tours are all my ideas," she told *Teen Beat* magazine. "It's very important to me to have a say in what's happening with the tour. I don't just want to go out there and be like, 'Well, here I am!' I want to know that I really had something to do with it."

A Living Doll!

Even Britney was caught by surprise when she became one of the major "must-haves" of the holiday season, but she shouldn't have been too, too shocked—after all, in pop music, you know you've made it major when you get turned into a doll!

In September 1999, Play-Along Toys introduced the Britney Spears doll—and before you could say ". . . Baby One More Time," it was one of the biggest selling toys of the year.

The doll, which stands eleven inches tall like a standard Barbie doll, represented Britney in each of her first three videos. For ". . . Baby One More Time," the doll was dressed in a short plaid skirt, white top, and thigh-high stockings; for the "Sometimes" doll, a mini-version of Brit's eye-catching white crop top and sweat pants was created; and the "Drive Me Crazy" doll wore a bright, glitzy green tube top and tight black pants. Each doll came fully equipped with all the tiny accessories needed to make a doll's life easier—a mini-microphone, mini-hairbrush, and mini-backpack, for example!

Britney was truly flattered to see herself represented in doll form and she was psyched that so many young fans wanted a Brit doll of their very own to play with and dress up. And

Britney knew she had to give the doll the ultimate thumbs-up when her little sister, Jamie Lyn, started playing with one. "I go home and my sister is playing with my Barbie doll," Britney told *16* magazine. "I'm like, oooh, that's soooo weird! But it's fun too. So much of what I do is hard work, and so serious—it's nice to be able to enjoy something fun like this."

And the Awards Keep Coming!

Of course, another one of the "fun things" that Britney got to do in 1999 was attend a bunch of awards show ceremonies—which meant plenty of dressing up, something Brit totally loves to do. But even more fun than getting gussied up in gorgeous gowns, meeting other ultra-famous celebs, and performing live for millions of people is winning an award or two—and that's something Britney got to experience over and over again.

The Luck of the Irish!

On November 11, 1999, Britney traveled to Dublin, Ireland, for the MTV Europe Music Awards. Britney looked totally sleek and chic in her black ensemble, and she really wowed the crowd with her energetic, powerhouse performance. But Britney was totally floored when she heard her name announced four times! Brit took home an award for Best Female Artist (beating out hip-hop queen Lauryn Hill, and Brit's own idol, Madonna); Best Pop (winning over the Backstreet Boys and Ricky Martin); Best Breakthrough Artist (taking that title from fellow nominees Jennifer Lopez and Eminem); and Best Pop Song for ". . . Baby One More Time," (Madonna, TLC, and the Backstreet Boys all went home empty handed when Britney snagged that award). The always gracious, always modest Britney was visibly blown away by her wins—it was a total MTV Europe Music Awards record, since no other artist had ever won more. "I can't believe it," she told reporters backstage. "I'm so honored by all this, and I want to send all my love to all my European fans."

Viva Las Vegas!

A few weeks later, Britney was back in the spotlight—this time, under the neon spotlights of Las Vegas, where she attended the Billboard Music Awards. For this glittery and glamorous occasion, Britney chose to wear a shimmery pink gown that gave off its own silver light every time she took a step in her matching silver sandals.

Once again, Britney was the big winner of the night, winning four of the coveted awards. She was honored as Billboard Magazine's Female Artist of the Year, New Artist of the Year, Female Album Artist of the Year, and Female Hot 100 Singles Artist of the Year.

Britney shared the stage with some pretty major musical talent—Ricky Martin, the Backstreet Boys, country trio the Dixie Chicks, and Mariah Carey were all honored at the star-studded event.

After the awards ceremony, Britney graciously stepped backstage to face the questions of newspaper reporters from all over the country. She talked a lot of the sacrifices her family had made to help her achieve her goals. "My father and my family—financially, we weren't always stable," she told reporters. "Yet no matter what, my family was always supportive, one hundred percent. When my mother first brought me to New York, when I was starting my career, we had hard times. We were lonely for the family. And my mom—I had my little sister, and that was unheard of in a small town, to move to New York. Everyone had something to say about that! But my mom always told me, if you ever get tired of this, or lonely and you want to go home, baby, we're going to do that."

Britney was also praised as a trailblazer, a pioneer of sorts, who opened the doors for so many other young performers. Super pop singers like Christina Aguilera, Mandy Moore, Jessica Simpson, and others all owe a big "thank you" to Britney, because her success helped make it possible for others to get their big musical breaks. Typically modest, Britney brushed off the compliment, but she did acknowledge that she'd worked very hard to get where she was—she would definitely not be a one-hit wonder! "Sometimes, because I'm always surrounded by adults, I feel a little bit older than other girls my age—but that's also because I've been doing this for so long," Britney told *Tiger Beat* magazine. "I've been building my career since I was little. So I know how much hard work it takes to get to the top in this business—it's not an easy thing at all."

After all the excitement of the awards show, Britney was back to being a typical teenager again, taking in the sights, sounds, and hot neon lights of Las Vegas. "It's not like I can gamble or anything," Britney told reporters backstage at the Billboard Music Awards. "I just like walking around with my friends, looking at everything—that's my favorite thing to do!"

All-American Girl!

In December 1999, Britney learned that she'd have to go shopping for a brand-new ball gown, because "Cinderella" Spears had been invited to another awards show, the American Music Awards. Once again, Britney topped the list of nominations—Britney, Whitney Houston, and Shania Twain received three nods apiece.

Miss Brit was nominated for Favorite Female Pop/Rock Artist (along with Whitney and Shania); Favorite Pop/Rock Album (other nominations went to the Backstreet Boys' *Millennium* and Santana's *Supernatural*); and Favorite New Pop/Rock Artist (up against Jennifer Lopez and Kid Rock). The award show aired on ABC-TV on January 17, 2000, and, lo and behold, Britney won the award for Favorite New Pop/Rock Artist. Way to go, Brit!

Some artists might get a little bigheaded with so many accolades and awards, but not Britney—she remains the sweet, grounded young girl she always was. "I think it's fun to get dressed up and win awards," she told *Teen Machine* magazine. "I'd be lying if I said I didn't like to win—it's nice to receive that kind of validation for your work. But that's not what it's all about. The really wonderful thing about this business is performing, doing the music, and being there for the fans. That's what I really love."

Movie (and TV!) Star in the Making!

Britney's never been shy about letting the world know that she's got future goals that go way beyond singing. She's determined to follow her dreams, and do some moonlighting in acting.

Although there's been a lot of talk about Britney appearing on *Dawson's Creek,* there have been no further developments regarding that show. But you gotta know Britney's not just sitting around waiting for things to hap-

pen—she's making things happen for herself.
Columbia Tri-Star (the company that produces
Dawson's Creek) is working on a TV series in
which Britney would star, and she's guest starring on several shows, like *The Simpsons* (she
appears as herself, in cartoon form) and *Beverly
Hills 90210*. "It's sometimes hard to find the
time to do everything," she admitted to *16*
magazine. "But I really want to try everything!"

And everything includes making a movie—
something she's already done! Britney appears
(along with 'N Sync) in the movie *Jack of All
Trades*, a film produced by "Big Poppa" Lou
Pearlman, of Trans Con Studios in Orlando,
Florida. In this movie she has a tiny role as a
flight attendant, but Britney is definitely dreaming of bigger movie roles—though not neces-
sarily the leading lady roles currently being
played by Gwyneth Paltrow and Drew
Barrymore. "I'd be scared to have that much
pressure on me," she told *Teen People* magazine. "It would be fun to do a teen movie—
maybe a supporting role, where I could show
my acting ability."

And of course, when you ask Brit who her
dream leading man would be, the answer is
always the same. "Ben Affleck," she told *TV
Guide*. "Definitely."

Her Royal Britney?

Although she's been paired with 'N Sync's

Justin Timberlake and Boyz-N-Girlz United's Rob Carrico, Britney says she's still a single girl in search of Mr. Right—and you might be totally shocked to hear Britney describe her dream man. "I like them with long hair, and really grungy," she told *TV Guide*. "Like rockers! Is that not crazy?"

It also doesn't sound like the real Prince Charming—Prince William of England—but the young royal and the princess of pop may be meeting one day soon. The 411? Prince William expressed an interest in Britney, and when she heard, she quickly sent him pictures and a letter. Wills has already invited Brit out to a party, but she had to stand him up! (Actually, she had to work!) It looks like the pair might just have a date on Valentine's Day, 2000. Could Britney be Her Royal Highness Britney one day? Stranger things have happened! And you know Brit would make one fine princess indeed.

And a New Album on the Way!

Of course, the one thing all true-blue Brit fans want to know is: "When will Britney release her second album?" The answer is, "Sooner than you think!"

Britney's as-yet-untitled album is due in record stores on May 18, 2000, and you'd better believe she's way excited about it. She started working on it in mid-1999, and surrounded herself with supertalented producers Max

Martin and Mutt Lange (who's produced two albums for his awesomely talented wife, Shania Twain). And she's hoping that this second album will show off a whole other side of Brit. "It's still pop music, but it's a little funkier," she told MTV News. "It's more 'now,' the music is 'now.' I want the album to be edgier—maybe with more of an R&B feel."

Britney's already worked on one of those 'now' songs—a beautiful ballad called "Don't Let Me Be the Last to Know." "With the first album, I didn't get to really show off my voice," she told MTV News. "The songs were great, but they weren't that challenging. This song is going to surprise people in the best possible way."

Right now, Britney is still busy putting the final touches on the album—and you might be surprised at some of the things she's considering adding to her CD! "I'd love to do a duet with someone totally unexpected, someone you wouldn't normally put me with," she told *TV Guide*. "Like Aerosmith's Steven Tyler—something crazy like that. Wouldn't that be cool?"

What's really cool for Brit fans is that very soon they'll be able to get a brand-new album filled with new Britney music. And Brit knows that making music for her fans is really what it's all about. But she also hopes her fans will be open to a few changes along the way. "I hope I have a few surprises left," she told *Tiger Beat* magazine. "I want to be around for a long time, and that means I always have to bring my fans something new."

JACKIE ROBB is a freelance writer based in the New York area. She also writes for a variety of teen magazines. She is currently working on several other books on young artists and performers, as well as a movie script and a play. She lives in New Jersey and is the biggest Britney fan who ever lived— besides you, of course!

DO IT YOURSELF!

Massage away tension, pain, and many other physical and mental disorders. There is nothing difficult or complicated about the zone therapy techniques described in this book. All but a few professional systems can be performed by anyone.

And zone therapy is perfectly safe. Our techniques may be used alone or in conjunction with conventional medical procedures. Of course, you should always consult your physician in case of serious or persistent symptoms. You may find that zone therapy is just what the doctor ordered.

Just follow our easy instructions. You'll be amazed at the results!

D0681639

ZONE THERAPY

by Anika Bergson
and Vladimir Tuchak

PINNACLE BOOKS **NEW YORK**
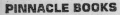

ZONE THERAPY

A Pinnacle Books edition, published for the first time anywhere.

First printing / September 1974

ISBN: 0-523-41860-4

Cover illustration by Bill Maughan

Printed in the United States of America

PINNACLE BOOKS, INC.
1430 Broadway
New York, New York 10018

20   19   18   17

CONTENTS

ZONE THERAPY

Introduction

This is, to our knowledge, the first book to bring together and collate all the diverse materials involving therapy by means of direct applied pressure on certain key parts of the human body, especially hands and feet. Many books in the past have presented excellent, though partial approaches to this unique science, but no effort has ever been made to synchronize and compare such diverse systems as acupuncture, foot and hand reflexology, and finger and tool massage therapy according to zones. Here then, for the first time, is a book that explains the different approaches, compares them, shows where they agree and where they disagree and, most important, gives the layman and the professional alike a step-by-step guide to the application of a group of systems which have been found to control and alleviate pain and disease in case after case.

The decision to undertake this project was based on the enthusiasm of our own experience with these simple and relatively unknown methods. After years of practicing zone therapy systems daily on a preventive basis, and also in the application of these methods for specific ailments on ourselves, our families, and willing and thankful friends, we felt it was time to pass such information on to the public. Friends who have benefited from our ministrations have been asking us for years to forego the easy life for a time and put down all we know in black and white. In doing so, of course, we have had to borrow from the work and the ideas of the many pioneers in such therapy. We cannot claim that these ideas are original with us; indeed, some of them go back to the ancient Egyptians, and others are the discoveries of the Chinese and the Japanese. The generic term *zone therapy* was coined by Dr. Edwin F. Bowers, M.D., an early associate of the great Dr. William H. FitzGerald, M.D., the first American to attempt to systematize the series of pressure relations he had found in the course of treating his patients and applying anesthesia without opiates in the first decades of this century.

For the sake of objectivity, we have refrained from cluttering the book with personal anecdotes and accounts of miraculous case history cures that do nothing for the reader but impose on his credibility. Instead, we sincerely urge the reader to practice whatever steps we outline as required to benefit his condition, and to practice them consistently and to the letter. If we indicate that four minutes of pressure must be applied on such and such a spot three times a day for so many weeks, we do not mean that two minutes every other day are going to do things for him. And, of course, in this life nothing can be really guaranteed. Even the most conscientious application of these methods might not yield the desired results, especially if the condition is tied to other pathological factors. We might establish a rule of thumb (no pun intended) that if this therapy does not work for a specific and clearly outlined condition, a physician should be consulted immediately, because it is obvious that the situation is such as to require prompt medical attention. We can go further and say that it is good common sense to always undertake the amelioration of any ailment in conjunction with a progressive medical person sympathetic to nonsurgical methods in medicine. Our great hope, naturally, is that in addition to reaching many among the general public suffering from those conditions mentioned in this book, we can bring these techniques to the attention of the medical profession so that, as in the days of Dr. Fitz-Gerald, some real work can again be undertaken by doctors to alleviate even the most serious of conditions through zone therapy systems.

We have sought to bring all pertinent material up to date and to discuss it in an intelligent manner. The avoidance of case history after case history was one way to achieve this. Too often, books on health written on the periphery of the medical profession have tended to sound like the work of quacks, with their fanatical belief in their own narrow and unscientific ways. These books are chatty, repetitive, sometimes confusing, and usually chockfull of unproved statements and facile explanations. The truth is that, to this day, no one knows why this type of therapy works at all. In recent years the West has finally accepted the irrefutable proofs of acupuncture healing in many areas of disease, much to the discomfort of those souls who who can only believe in more "logical" ways. Soviet advances in Kirlian photography have revolutionized the approach to biology and pathology. Such findings, right before the eyes of the world in color photography, support the ancient Chinese concept of Ch'i energy, and take the use of pressure or needles applied on key areas of the body out of the realm of magic. Our work cannot any longer be relegated by anybody to the dustbin of an old wives' tale. Still, the fact remains that zones and meridians have not been explained to the satisfaction of science. The thing works, but no one knows how. Nobody knows for sure why proper pressure below the big toe affects the spinal column at shoulder level. All attempts to say that "crystal deposits" at the nerve endings of the foot are dissolved by pressure, thereby activating blood circulation, are mere conjecture. They are an insult to the scientifically trained person, tending to antagonize him and make him dismiss this whole body of knowledge as pure wishful thinking. We shall offer no pseudoscientific explanations whatever; instead, we shall take a purely pragmatic approach. What works, works, and if it alleviates human suffering, we suggest that it should be practiced whether or not we understand it from the point of view of established science. Someday the actual reasons will be discovered, and we venture to say that they will make as much sense as any other scientific fact. But until then we must limit ourselves to the humble task of showing how to obtain relief from dozens of painful conditions, and that alone.

This is truly a do-it-yourself book. There is nothing complicated or difficult about the techniques in these systems of therapy. Whether you have a professional or just a friend treat you, or you are entirely alone, there are no techniques discussed here that are beyond the grasp and mastery of the layman. A few exceptions are clearly indicated as such and are included in this book for the sake of completeness. For example, throat and nasal massage with the aid of medical tools are mentioned at the appropriate places so that interested doctors may begin to practice again what doctors such as Dr. FitzGerald and Dr. Bowers knew and practiced fifty years ago with great success. Aside from these professional techniques, everything else can be undertaken with complete confidence by the most untrained of persons. We have taken care to go into every detail, the description and portrayal of zones, the comparisons, the precise way to apply pressure, the use of such tools as clothespins, rubber bands, combs, and pencil erasers, and the amount of time required for each operation. There is no way that an error can be made if our instructions are followed. Besides, there is no known danger in practicing these systems even where one fails to do it properly. Body reflexes are such that their manipulation will operate for the benefit of their correlative zones even if we fail to zero in on a malady.

Many charts accompany the text and take the guesswork out of finger and tool massage. With one glance at the appropriate illustration, the neophyte is ready to bring physical relief to himself or those around him. These manipulations are so simple that they can be undertaken standing, sitting, or lying in bed, whichever is the most comfortable.

An important feature of this work is the arrangement and discussion according to areas and ailments to be treated. Most books on the subject treat these things in a less direct fashion, preferring to discuss several things at once or suddenly coming forth with gratuitous advice on other matters, with the result that the reader has to wade through reams of material before coming upon and understanding that which most interests him. In this book, beginning with Chapter Three, zone therapy systems are broken down alphabetically by disease or area of discomfort. This allows quick reference. If you suffer from headaches you can open the book to the chapter on headaches;

you won't find anything there about the gall-bladder to confuse you and delay the treatment.

Naturally, a book devoted to the study of so mysterious and together a thing as the human body could not end on a divisive note. When a part or an organ of the body has been suffering from a pathological condition, it doesn't take long before affecting other parts and organs. An ounce of prevention is therefore worth a pound of regret. Consequently, the reader's attention is directed to the last chapter, Ten Minutes to Health. There he will find a discussion of preventive medicine and of the simple therapy he can follow to retain and improve his health. It is ironic that millions of people practice muscle exercises religiously each morning upon arising, as if their bodies were entirely made up of muscle and nothing but muscle. Now, we are not for one minute suggesting that such an excellent practice be discontinued. On the contrary, muscle tone is one of the keys to general body health. Unfortunately for these people, it is far from being the whole story. Such exercises should be backed up by the equally important exercise of glands and internal organs. Only zone therapy systems can reach these all-important centers of life. It is entirely up to the individual just how healthy he wishes to be once he is acquainted with the secrets of radiant well-being. The exercise we have devised for either morning or evening application take no longer than ten minutes to perform. It may yield dividends measurable in years of happy life and contented old age.

It is primarily as a preventive and additional therapy that this book is offered to the general public. No claim is made by the authors that any technique described here will work in any specific case. Indeed, not even medical science can claim to cure each and every case that comes to its attention. Zone therapy systems are meant to be applied side by side with the thoughtful ministrations of your own physician; they should have his supervision and meet with his approval. Zone therapy systems are a boost to conventional curative methods as practiced by the medical profession, not something opposed to or at variance with its practice. What can be said to be true is that the conscientious application of the techniques described in this book can bring relief of harmful tensions and other dangerous psychosomatic factors. Where this, plus the relief of pain, is achieved, we are well on the road to recovery and the defeat of disease.

The stark simplicity of these wonderful methods stands in direct and dramatic contrast to the very nature of disease and those stubborn and depressing psychological conditions which disease brings in its wake. Zone therapy systems cannot possibly be detrimental if followed correctly. They can be amazingly, miraculously effective.

1

History, Ancient and Recent

There is almost no doubt that some very ancient civilizations knew how to cure the diseases of man in ways that would certainly amaze us, and make us grope for adjectives other than crude or primitive. Chance and experimentation with massage, pressure, herbs, and diet throughout thousands of years must have led in a good many cases to great finds, to discoveries that helped prove a boon to mankind. Then, of course, these civilizations decayed or were overrun, and their medical secrets were lost or destroyed. Perhaps some survive to this day, and each one of us has scoffed at what we deprecatingly call old wives' tales, handed down by word of mouth since time immemorial, not sure that they work and unwilling to try them. Willful cases involving the destruction of knowledge, such as the tragic burning of the library at Alexandria or the destruction of a wonderful body of Indian herbal lore by the Spaniards, are incalculable historical losses. Events of this nature can be blamed for the little we know, for instance, of how the ancient

Egyptians practiced medicine, or how the Incas managed brain surgery. In those cases where we are believed to have better records, such as with Chinese folk medicine, we discover that the curtain of fog parts to reveal not so much facts as myths about its origins. This cannot be avoided, for ancient man saw all events impinging on his destiny within the context of magic and religion. The concepts of traditional Chinese medicine and acupuncture are intimately connected with the philosophy of the *Tao Te Ching*, or Book of the Way. Especially important concepts are those of yin and yang, and the notion that man—as indeed all things —exists in a vast and indivisible whole which is constantly interreacting. The ancient Chinese sages believed that for man to maintain mental and physical health he had to enter into a harmonious relationship with everything else; he had to fit into a world of correspondences where the twin principles, yin and yang, ruled "the ten thousand things." Yin represents the negative force, the quiescent, female principle; and yang the positive, active, male principle. Just how these two principles are balanced in one's body would explain to the Chinese sage one's state of health. For instance, where yang is predominant, the body tends to be overheated, fevers have a chance to rise, the person is tense and irritable.

It should be obvious that with such an all-encompassing approach, even the most ancient Chinese doctors could do much for their patients; certainly much more than their European counterparts of the Middle Ages. Chinese history is replete with the names of great doctors and their cures. Magnificent finds, such as the circulation of the blood, are mentioned in the *Huang-ti nei ching*, or The Yellow Emperor's Book of Internal Medicine, some 4,000 years ago.

Acupuncture, conservatively estimated to be more than 2,000 years old, is based on the concept that the human body has an internal set of channels—or meridians, as these are now called—with 365 points where the channels surface onto the skin. These meridians are places where control on yin and yang can best be exercised and effected by the insertion of needles.

Up to the turn of this century, acupuncture was practiced exclusively in the Orient; yet, curiously enough, Western doctors in the nineteenth century had begun to discover hitherto hidden secrets about the human body that were not too unlike what the Chinese knew empirically. The earliest to do so was the Swede Pehr Henrik Ling. In 1834, Ling noticed that pains emanating from certain organs were reflected in certain areas of the skin with no direct relation to those organs. Other students followed, including the English neurologist Sir Henry Head; the treatment zones he discovered came to be known as "Head's zones." Therapeutic anesthesia had been born. Today, we are beginning to find how these zones bear relationships

11

to acupuncture, even though the complexity of the nervous system is one that will continue to baffle scientists looking for clear-cut "reasons" for all this seeming nonsense. But research scientists are in agreement that, when all is said and done, yin and yang polarities correspond to our Western theory of the sympathetic and parasympathetic nervous system.

The recent work done in the Soviet Union, especially by S. D. Kirlian and V. Kh. Kirlian, is of outstanding importance because it tends to prove the reality of meridians and, by implication, the entire theory of zone therapy systems. As far back as the 1890s, a Russian engineer named Yakov Narkevich-Todko was experimenting with electrographic photographs. These were obtained by using electrical discharges to photograph weird bluish flames emanating from living bodies. These bluish discharges have been known since Biblical times, and are most familiar to sailors because they are often seen around the mastheads and the riggings of ships. This phenomenon is commonly called St. Elmo's fire. It occurs on land as well, and records exist of people out West reporting opening their iron stoves only to see a big bluish ball of fire come tumbling out. There is a simple explanation for this: the stove chimney probably attracted static electricity, available whenever there are electrical storms in the air. The electricity, accumulating in the bowels of the stove, came out as a ball of flame.

Stranger still, cases have been reported where human beings have seemed to act as storage batteries for this kind of electricity. Anyone touching them would receive a painful shock.

In any event, as Czechoslovakian parapsychologists suggest, a kind of biological energy, which they have termed bio-energy, is at work in a great deal of so-called psychic phenomena. This bio-energy is far more subtle than electromagnetic waves, and the way it operates within the human body is not yet known. It is there, of that we may be sure, but its relationship to the health of the person is still a puzzle to investigators. What we can assert is that this energy demands that our previous, simplistic, mechanical approach to bodily functions and interactions be expanded, as was Newtonian physics.

Experiments by the Kirlians demonstrate that photographs of the fingertips of an even-tempered man, as opposed to those of a tired, emotionally tense individual, differed not once but consistently as far as those mysterious flames are concerned; and such photographs have been published, showing graphically these remarkable differences. The fact inescapably emerges that living organisms are electrodynamic systems of great complexity, and the most subtle correlations exist between their parts.

As the Kirlians found out when they used their technique to photograph leaves, a healthy leaf will give a different image than an old or a dried-out one. Thus, the biological condition of an organism can be read in the same way that X-rays enable us to read skeletal conditions. From the point of view of preventive medicine, such "readings" will help diagnose conditions which could not otherwise be detected, or discovered as soon. One of the most interesting things that the Kirlians found out was that different parts of the human skin give off different colors. They state that the heart region gives off an intense blue, the forearm is greenish-blue, and the thigh olive green. During fear or illness the inherent color of an area changes. The flames that emanate from the skin are reported to differ; they are not uniform or even. Some come in the shape of points, others form coronas and flares of luminescent clusters that come in different colors. At some points on the skin blue and gold luminescences flare up suddenly. Could these be acupuncture points? Some of these flames leap from one point on the skin only to land on another, where they are absorbed. Scientists assume that these different performance patterns obey different biomechanical systems functioning in common, just as the different colors observed could emanate from different systems.

So complete is the biological entity from the point of view of these electrical systems that when a leaf with a section missing has been photographed, the flare patterns of the entire leaf continue to appear as if that part had not been removed at all and were still part and parcel of the leaf.

Perhaps enough has been said to convince the reader that the next few decades will bring revolutionary changes in the way we go about mending and helping the body back to health. New medical techniques will be used that are not even in their infancy at this point. But the importance of pressure therapy cannot be underestimated in this connection, and we should see a great development in the spread and sophistication with which zone massage is used in pathology as well as in preventive medicine.

Exciting as the prospect appears, we are still back at the stage of creeping doubts and official contention. The American doctors who pioneered zone therapy systems in the early part of this century had to wage an uphill fight not to be laughed out of town as simple charlatans. Even today, the notion of a doctor suggesting that you clench a plain aluminum comb in your hand for some minutes in order to relax you and relieve you of a case of lumbago is so preposterous-sounding that your first impulse is to laugh and go see the medical man next door. And yet, that is precisely what Dr. William FitzGerald was able to do on occasion, with brilliant results.

Dr. FitzGerald was an ear, nose, and throat specialist in Connecticut. He was a graduate of the University of Vermont, who worked in hospitals in Boston, London, and Vienna. He began to be interested in this new approach by observing that he could carry out minor operations on the nose and throat by replacing the cocaine used in those days to deaden pain with pressure on certain parts of the body. Looking into the matter further, he discovered that not all patients reacted alike to these pressures, and that some patients came to him and, either before or during the operation, would tense up or squeeze their hands in preparation for the ordeal they were expecting. In some cases, the tension along the hands was enough to anesthetize these persons. Soon, he had his dentist friends using his method of pressure application in order to perform their previously horrifyingly painful work. Hundreds and hundreds of patients were treated by these men at the dawn of zone therapy systems, some of them with truly amazing results. But, of course, even in the medical profession prejudice dies hard, and doctors by and large preferred to continue believing in their time-honored methods rather than experiment and find drugless solutions to human suffering

One man who was not afraid to look into the matter was Dr. Edwin F. Bowers, M.D., of New York, who took it upon himself to go and visit Dr. FitzGerald and observe for himself some of these cures that were the talk of professional circles. Dr. Bowers left convinced that there was something very important in those methods, and wrote an article in which he christened the budding science zone therapy.

16

Dr. FitzGerald evolved a theory that divided the human body longitudinally into five zones on the left and five zones on the right. We will be comparing these zones with the meridians of acupuncture in the next chapter, so it will suffice to mention here that these zones relate all parts of the body within each zone in such a way that any problem in one zone could conceivably be treated by pressure somewhere else within it. In this way, a problem with the left eye could react to pressure on the third toe of the left foot, since both these parts of the body lie within zone three. This is, naturally, an oversimplification, because relief will depend upon how and where exactly that toe is pressured, but the explanation has been given for the sake of presenting in capsule form the single most important element in zone therapy systems.

In view of all we have said relating to acupuncture and Kirlian photography, the reader will immediately understand the profound rightness of the theory which Dr. FitzGerald came upon, thanks to his sensitivity to human pain, a sensitivity that marked him as a true physician. Most methods of pressure therapy in the United States stem from the work of those two American pioneers, Dr. FitzGerald and Dr. Bowers, in addition to the incredibly successful practice of the Los Angeles doctor, George Starr White, M.D.

But enough of history. Let's get on with the

task of discovering a few secrets of the human body, and how we can put those secrets to work for us in relieving pain and assisting the curative powers of nature.

2

Of Feet and Hands, of Charts and Tools

A comparison of the chart designed by Dr. FitzGerald (see Figure 1) showing the body divided into five zones on the left and five on the right, with Master H'su Ch'ang's acupuncture meridians (Figure 2) will show how closely related the two approaches are to a general way of treating the human body and its ailments.

Acupuncture has developed a method of treating points where the meridians surface on the body by means of needles inserted at those points. Until recently, there was no scientific proof that these points were any different from any other area in the body, but Dr. Kim Bongham of North Korea has discovered "little groups of egg-shaped cells at acupuncture points which are united with one another by bundles of hollow tubular cells . . ." So there appears to be this "fourth system of communication—the others being nervous, vascular, and lymphatic."

Only further research will show just how zone therapy as applied to the feet and hands

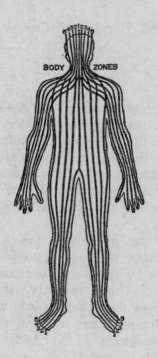

BODY ZONES

Figure 1.

20

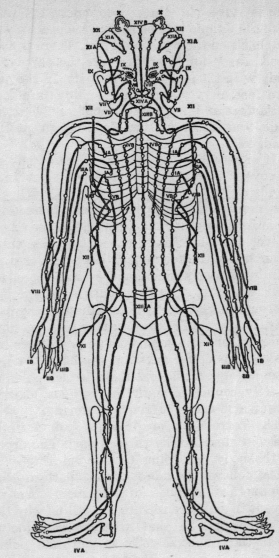

Figure 2.

21

works vis-à-vis these acupuncture centers. What is unique to zone therapy is precisely that emphasis on the hands and feet. There is a very good reason for this; these are the parts of the body with the least depth to them. In the hands and feet, nerves and nerve endings are forced to surface and are thus more accessible to massage and manipulation, leading to pressure analgesia.

If one studies the FitzGerald chart one soon discovers that the same reflexes exist in the hands as in the feet. However, specific points are more difficult to locate and therefore to treat in the human hand, because of the amount of work that the hand undertakes daily. On the other hand, the foot is kept in a tender condition by the very fact that we wear shoes. It is thus easier to treat the entire system by a thorough massage of the feet than in any other way. Readers will soon discover just how much more tender certain parts of their feet are than the corresponding parts on the hand. And the fascinating part is that those tender parts are directly connected with the various maladies from which one is currently suffering.

The correlation of pressure points in the feet and hands to the various parts and organs of the body according to the ten FitzGerald zones follows a more direct pattern than acupuncture methods of treatment. We will leave it to a future scientist to tell us why that is. Our guess is that whereas acupuncture treats those special cells at meridian points, zone therapy works more directly on nerve endings that are intimately connected with organs along the ten zones.

Leaving aside the more theoretical aspects, we would like at this point to discuss the various simple tools that may be used to relieve pain. Before doing so, however, the reader should study Figures 3 and 4, for these charts give him a bird's-eye view of the zone areas in both the hands and the feet. We will be going into the ways to attack these pressure areas depending on the malady involved, but we suggest that the reader take the first practical step at this time and, chart in hand, follow or feel the various points indicated on both the hands and the feet. Pressure may be applied with the thumb. We venture to say that the average reader will be surprised to find how many areas respond with soreness when only a minimal amount of firm pressure is applied. That is one indication that the reader's health is not as abundant as it should be.

From time to time we will be suggesting a variety of simple tools that may be used in zone therapy. In addition to the all-important human thumb, which is generally the best tool, there will be times when a more incisive pressure will be required. The rubber eraser on a pencil is marvelous for just that kind of fine, in-depth massage required at times. The pioneers in zone therapy discovered early in the game that a more constant kind of pressure on the fingers of the hand worked wonders with

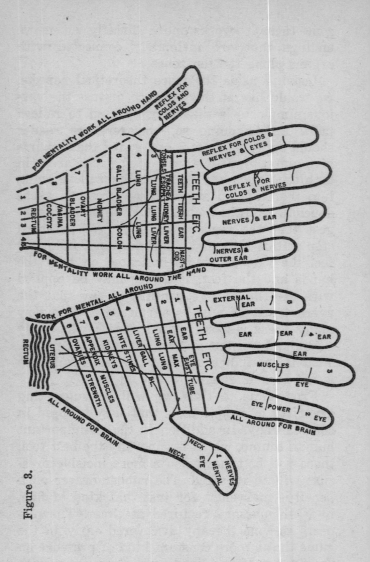

Figure 3.

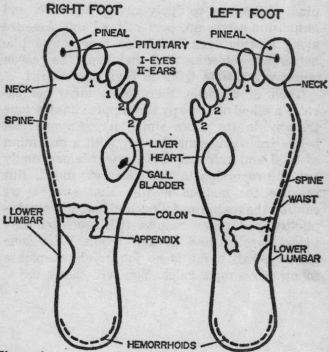

Figure 4.

RIGHT FOOT

PINEAL
PITUITARY
PINEAL
I-EYES
II-EARS
NECK
1
1
2
2
SPINE
LIVER
HEART
GALL
BLADDER
LOWER
LUMBAR
COLON
APPENDIX

LEFT FOOT

PINEAL
NECK
1
2
2
SPINE
WAIST
LOWER
LUMBAR

HEMORRHOIDS

some ailments. Pragmatists that they were, they soon found a perfect solution for that in the form of rubber bands. These are wound around specific joints of specific fingers, as will be indicated in due course. In addition, clothespins can be used to apply strong pressure, and aluminum combs are perfect for hand pressure along a wide area. All these may sound like homemade remedies, and they are. The reason why we advocate them is that they work!

Tools or no tools, there is no other comparable method of therapy that approximates zone therapy in its utter simplicity. Anyone can begin practicing zone therapy with a minimum of trial and error, and the rewards are really out of proportion to the effort expended. But because the method is just that simple, we caution the reader to follow our instructions explicitly for the best results. It is much too easy to get careless and do half a job. With zone therapy, half a job is no job at all, so please follow our simple rules. You will thank us!

3

Anemia

Anemia is due to lack of iron in the blood; it can cause serious trouble if left to run its course. Women, who need more iron than men, are more prone to anemia.

The organ most directly involved with anemia is the spleen, because it is there that iron is stored until needed by the blood. If you discover that the area of the spleen in your foot has any tenderness, you are probably somewhat anemic. Fortunately, improvement can be rapid unless you have pernicious anemia, in which case the cure will be slower.

If you refer to Figure 5, you will see that the spleen lies under the heart, on the left side of the body. Consequently, only the left foot, at the appropriate place, should be massaged.

The spleen is a soft but brittle organ somewhat long and flattened, whose size and weight is liable to vary at different periods in life. The adult spleen is usually about five inches in length and weighs about seven ounces.

Because the spleen has a lot to do with both the large and small intestines, soreness at the

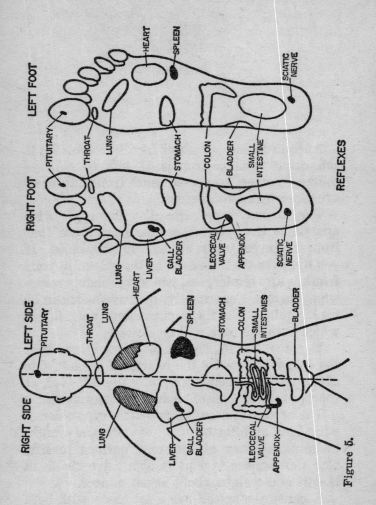

LEFT FOOT

HEART
SPLEEN
SCIATIC NERVE
PITUITARY
THROAT
LUNG
STOMACH
COLON
BLADDER
SMALL INTESTINE

RIGHT FOOT

LUNG
HEART
LIVER
GALL BLADDER
ILEOCECAL VALVE
APPENDIX
SCIATIC NERVE

REFLEXES

LEFT SIDE

RIGHT SIDE

PITUITARY
THROAT
LUNG
HEART
LUNG
LIVER
GALL BLADDER
ILEOCECAL VALVE
APPENDIX
SPLEEN
STOMACH
COLON
SMALL INTESTINES
BLADDER

Figure 5.

28

zone in the foot where the spleen reflects might not indicate an anemic condition one hundred percent of the time. It could actually mean a disturbance in the colon. However, if you feel low in energy or if a doctor has actually diagnosed anemia, then you can assume that those other connections do not apply.

In cases of marked anemia, the spleen area will be extremely sore, and massage of the area should be limited to a few minutes a day. Use the thumb in a circular motion directly over the sore spot.

In addition to massage, a diet rich in minerals, as directed by a competent nutritionist, will assist in recovery.

4

Anesthesia

This chapter will be of more interest to doctors and dentists than to the layman, but the subject is of enough importance to warrant appearing in a do-it-yourself type of book such as this.

We should begin by pointing out that there is a difference between zone therapy and what can be termed direct nerve blocking or pressure analgesia. This latter consists—as the term implies—of pressure directly over the nerve supplying a certain area. Obviously, this is quite different from a system that applies pressure in a zone far removed from the area that one is treating.

That both approaches work can be proven by experimentation. Pressure directly on the dental nerve will block sensations normally felt on the teeth involved with that nerve. With zone therapy, pressure on certain fingers or toes in the same zone will inhibit the pain in that same tooth or teeth.

If the reader will refer back to Figure 1, he will see, for instance, that both the big toe and the thumb are in zone one, and that zone one is the most central of the zones and involves the nose, front teeth, center of the tongue, and so on down the body. Similarly, the various toes and fingers affect corresponding parts of the body. Common sense will show that the middle ear, for instance, is in zone four. An organ like the liver lies in all five zones on the right side of the body, and in zones one, two, and sometimes three on the left side; a good practitioner of zone therapy makes sure that he covers all possible zones for a given organ when massaging. Another point we might make at this time is that in treating any of the internal organs it is a good idea to tackle both the anterior and posterior zone simultaneously (see Figures 6 and 7).

Empirical knowledge of anesthesia has existed for a long time. Everyone knows that a blow to the pit of the stomach will render a person unconscious. Fighters are aware that a blow to the temple or at a certain angle to the jaw will produce similar results. In the old days, before anesthesia, surgeons sometimes experimented with pressure along the nerve centers in the neck. The results obtained were positive; however, no one knew how long the patient would remain unconscious after the operation!

Pain anywhere in the first zone can be treated and made to disappear, sometimes for good, through pressure on the entire surface of the big toe's first joint. If the pressure is ap-

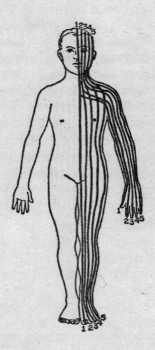

Figure 6.

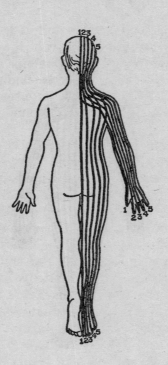

Figure 7.

plied only on the upper surface, the effect will be felt along the front of the body. Conversely, pressure on the under side of the big toe will bring relief along the first zone in back of the body.

Strong pressure on the end of the big toe or the tip of the thumb controls the whole first zone. Similar pressure on the tips of the other fingers will affect the corresponding zones in the body. Lateral pressure on either fingers or toes will affect the lateral boundaries of the body.

Partial anesthesia can also be obtained by pressure on a bony surface. This pressure may be applied with a sharp-pointed applicator or with the nails of the thumb or fingers.

Pressure applied through rubber bands wound on fingers, toes, wrist, or ankle will also produce anesthesia. Even the knees and elbows can be involved in this method so that pain in several zones can be eliminated. One point that we must make, however, is that if the pain increases after this kind of treatment, pathological symptoms of another nature may be involved in the zones affected.

Pressure should average from half a minute to four minutes or longer, depending on the severity of the pain.

Dentists should know that pressure on the big toe may anesthetize the incisor region enough for the painless extraction of incisors and bicuspids. The dentist may supplement this pressure himself by applying pressure directly on the lip or cheek and on the jaw. The second zone usually includes the cuspids and biscuspids. The third zone governs the two molars and the fourth zone the third molar teeth. Pressure applied with the thumb or a cautery contact on the upper or lower jaw will relieve pain by zone.

Dr. FitzGerald gives further advice to dentists as follows: "Pressure or cautery contact on the buccal surface of the jaws control anterior sections of zones, one, two, three, four, and often five; and pressure or cautery contact on lingual surface of jaws control posterior sections of above zones. Zones four and five usually merge in the head. Pressure with the thumb or finger on inferior dental and lingual nerves, at inferior dental foramen, will often anesthetize that half of the jaw, and to a greater extent the entire half of the body on side compressed.

"Because of the anastomosis of nerves at the median line of the jaw, this pressure occasionally causes an anesthesia of a part or even the whole of the opposite side of the jaw, but this is the only instance thus far noticed where anesthesia through pressure crosses the median line of the body."

A mouth in which there is normal occlusion by the natural teeth is a great asset, since the entire organism can be made to relax by simple biting pressure held for two or three minutes. Pain in any zone can sometimes be relieved by this simple expedient; occasionally, even anesthesia may be induced where true occlusion occurs and the pressure is held firmly for a few minutes.

These methods will never produce soreness of the jaw. Quite the contrary, in cases where operations have been carried out or where hemorrhage has taken place, pressure with the thumb or fingers will overcome or lessen the difficulty.

In conclusion, we might sum up this entire question of anesthesia by saying that a practiced doctor or dentist can anesthetize a patient from the head to the feet by pressure on resistant surfaces of the head and/or by pressure on the extremities. Individuals may obtain analgesic effects by means of pressure with their teeth if they possess good occlusion, and by pressure on specific fingers.

It should be pointed out that whereas the right amount of pressure is of great value to the organism, too much pressure, or for too long a period, is harmful and leads to weakness and irritability. Tight shoes, belts, corsets, or collars will invariably have a detrimental effect upon bodily health.

5

Appendicitis

The reflex for the appendix and the ileocecal valve, which connects the small intestine to the large, is located slightly to the right of center on the right foot (see Figure 8). The appendix is a narrow tube from three to six inches long; it has no fixed position. Pressure with the left thumb on the spot indicated can soon tell you

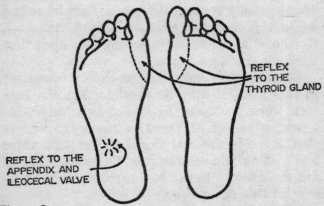

REFLEX TO THE THYROID GLAND

REFLEX TO THE APPENDIX AND ILEOCECAL VALVE

Figure 8.

if there is a tendency to congestion of the appendix.

Recoveries from appendicitis have been achieved through the massaging of the reflex for this organ. However, in case of an acute attack, a physician should be seen at once. You may massage the appendix reflex until he sees you since this action can only benefit the situation, but bear in mind that it won't be a solution.

Since the appendix is a small organ, a little exploring with the thumb will be necessary before you can zero in on it. Press in with the tip of the thumb below the foot's center and slightly toward its outer edge. Now move the thumb in a rolling motion. If you detect some pain there, it might be worthwhile to switch to a pencil with a rubber eraser and explore the exact location of the pain so that the massage will center on the source of the trouble. Massage only for a few seconds, then let it rest while you massage another part of the foot. Keep coming back for a few seconds each time until all soreness is gone.

Because the organs are so closely connected in this area, it may be possible that the ileocecal valve, not your appendix, is affected. Interestingly enough, there is reason to believe that there is a connection between this valve and some kinds of allergies. Cases of allergies are reported to have been cured through massage of this reflex zone.

Whatever the trouble, massage in this area will help relieve symptoms that might be accumulating and which would cause serious trouble later on. The abolition of soreness in this area through careful massage represents a wonderful case of preventive medicine.

6

Arthritis

Arthritis is so complex a condition that not even medical science is able to cope with it. There are many theories about it but nothing is known for certain. Because of this fact, we can only suggest a couple of methods that might bring amelioration.

The first is based on the idea that arthritis is caused by an accumulation of poisons and acids, as well as calcium, and that this is due to faulty functioning of the digestive system. It would do no harm for the person suffering from arthritis to concentrate then on massaging that area of the feet directly connected to the stomach and intestines (see Figure 4), remembering that one cannot expect results with arthritis in days or weeks. Experimentation with the massage in the feet reflexes of the several internal organs might yield an unexpected result. This result might be preceded by an apparent worsening of the arthritic condition as the poisons retained by the system are released through the massage.

The other approach is to attack those reflexes

43

in the feet connected to the endocrine glands. After all, these are the glands that supply the body with the regulatory factors and substances that bring health. A condition such as arthritis may signify that one gland or another is not delivering or functioning properly. Please study Figure 9 and see that you massage the reflexes to all of them for at least two weeks. The thumb is the best instrument for this and several minutes a day will suffice. When you find a particularly tender spot give it a good massage and come back to it later on. Do one foot at a time and be sure to massage any tender area regardless of its connection to a specific organ. Pain in the foot is always an indication of disorder in the body, so no soreness should be disregarded.

When massaging the parathyroid reflexes, you might wish to transfer to the use of a rubber eraser at the tip of a pencil, since it is necessary to really hit those small spots in the feet, and the thumb is too broad in this case.

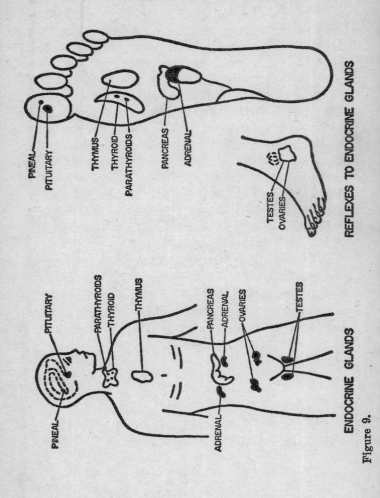

REFLEXES TO ENDOCRINE GLANDS

PINEAL
PITUITARY
THYMUS
THYROID
PARATHYROIDS
PANCREAS
ADRENAL
TESTES
OVARIES

ENDOCRINE GLANDS

PITUITARY
PARATHYROIDS
THYROID
THYMUS
PANCREAS
ADRENAL
OVARIES
TESTES
PINEAL
ADRENAL

Figure 9.

45

7

Asthma, Bronchitis, Coughs

Asthmatic conditions are best treated by means of pressure on the floor of the mouth. In fact, the old pioneers of zone therapy had many nearly miraculous cures to report by using this direct method of attack. For this purpose, a medical probe that is cotton-tipped works best, and it should be used beneath the root of the tongue.

Severe bronchial asthma may also be relieved by pressing strongly on the first and third zones of the tongue (the tongue contains all ten zones) with a tongue depressor. In fact, patients may help themselves by biting the tongue as hard as possible, holding it between the teeth for several minutes at a time, three or four times daily.

Persons suffering from asthma would do well to have their teeth, throat, and pharynx checked by a medical doctor, since it is a fact that some asthmatic conditions are not resolved until defects in these areas are cleared up.

Some authorities in the field insist that asthma can be treated through zone therapy by attacking the reflex for the adrenal glands (see Figure 9). They base their theory on the fact that since adrenalin injections can help break up an attack of asthma, it should follow that activation of the adrenal glands might just be the thing that will bring on relief of this condition. Asthmatic patients with soreness showing at the point of this reflex will do well to massage it several times a day.

Dr. FitzGerald had several suggestions, some of which can only be undertaken by a physician. In the first place, he suggested traction of the soft palate with a finger or a hook probe. In some cases he found that the use of rubber bands wound around all the fingers or toes, from ten to fifteen minutes several times daily, brought improvement. One of his strangest methods was to press with the index finger against the front teeth of the patient.

For bronchitis, a doctor may pass a cotton-tipped probe through the nose to the epipharynx. When he has touched the exact location, the patient should feel a sensation in his throat that corresponds to the zones of the bronchi affected. Such pressure should be maintained from one to three minutes.

A less extreme method involves the use of the two index fingers to stretch the lips. This should be done several times daily. Coughs may be alleviated by this simple process.

The central zones affected by asthma or cough can also be treated by tongue-pulling (see

Figure 10.

Figure 10). The tongue may be twisted from side to side as well.

Zone therapy is most directly involved in bronchial cases by the manipulation of the foot reflexes for the lungs and bronchial tubes. These reflexes are located at the pads of the feet, directly beneath the toes (see Figure 11). Since the lungs take up quite a bit of space in the chest, it is not unusual to find that their reflexes in each foot take up so much room. To massage, hold the right foot with the left hand and use the right hand to rub the entire reflex area. Use a circular, rolling motion. Massage of the whole lung area will benefit the bronchial tubes. And since the bronchial tubes are buried deep in the chest, it may be necessary for you to massage

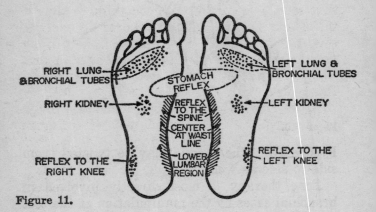

RIGHT LUNG & BRONCHIAL TUBES

LEFT LUNG & BRONCHIAL TUBES

STOMACH REFLEX

RIGHT KIDNEY

LEFT KIDNEY

REFLEX TO THE SPINE

CENTER AT WAIST LINE

REFLEX TO THE RIGHT KNEE

LOWER LUMBAR REGION

REFLEX TO THE LEFT KNEE

Figure 11.

thoroughly and deeply; a light probe may not even reveal soreness.

Whooping coughs and other types of cough may be handled as follows: A cotton-tipped probe is applied to the back of the throat (the post-pharyngeal wall) and held firmly there for several minutes. The throat may develop some soreness from this type of treatment but that soon passes, and the good thing is that it takes very few such treatments for an average condition to clear up. This applies to any cough originating in the respiratory passages in that zone (and not, of course, to something like a tubercular cough).

A less complicated method of curing a cough is to grasp the tongue resolutely (see Figure 10) and give it a long and hard pull, holding it out as long as the patient can stand it.

The use of the probe might scare some people, although we recommend it as the quickest cure of all. Less dramatic results can also be obtained by the application of firm pressure on the front part of the tongue and on the floor of the mouth under the tongue. In addition, moderately tight rubber bands may be worn on the thumbs and first fingers of the hands for five and even ten minutes at a time, several times a day.

Holding the bridge of the nose with the first finger and thumb and applying strong pressure for several minutes is also helpful, especially if there is a frontal headache accompanying the cough.

8

Back Problems, Lumbago

Practically everybody complains at one time or another of pains in the back. Back problems are almost endemic to man and are attributed to the fact that, back in the forgotten past, he changed his way of walking and straightened up, placing a great amount of stress on the small of the back. Be that as it may, zone therapy can help immensely to restore health to any part of the back faced with problems of pinched nerves and the congestion brought on by muscular contraction.

Since the spinal column is in the exact center of the body, it follows that the reflex for it lies along the first zone of each foot (see Figure 12), going lengthwise from the big toe to the heel. If you understand that the toe itself stands for the head and that the center of the foot stands for the center of the back, and so forth, you will have no trouble in locating the exact spot to manipulate in reference to the pains along your back. People with problems in the lumbar region of the spine will follow the reflex down towards the heel until they can lo-

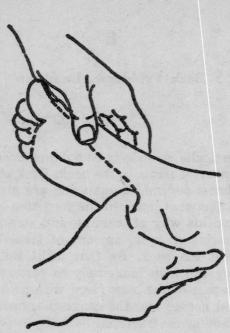

Figure 12.

cate tell-tale tenderness. When the problem area is located, begin your massage quite gently at first—spine reflexes are usually quite sore— and continue in this fashion until you can work the tenderness out.

The reflexes of the back may be massaged for any length of time you desire, unlike certain organs such as the liver, which must be handled with care.

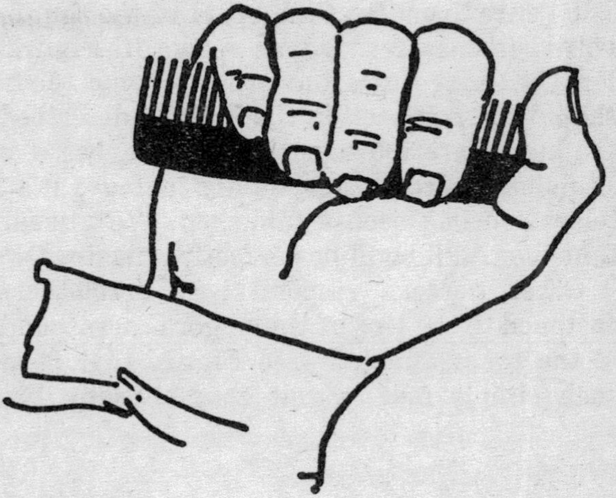

Figure 13.

Lumbago usually responds quite quickly to zone therapy, and cases of people doubled up with this sickness have been reported cured in one single treatment. Amazingly enough, the one tool that has been found the most beneficial is an ordinary aluminum comb, such as the kind that is used for dog-combing purposes (see Figure 13). The way to use it is to press the teeth of the comb against the inner surfaces of the fingers of each hand and, later, against the palms of the hands. For best results, such pressure must be maintained for ten or even twenty minutes. Persistent cases of lumbago may require workouts of the web between the thumb and first finger, and also the web between the first and second fingers of each hand.

Be sure to get the fleshy part of the thumb involved in the pressure, as shown in Figure 13. For the best results, the entire palm of the hand should be "combed" in the fashion described. If the hands are too sensitive at first, begin with slight pressure and gradually increase it when toleration has been established. We guarantee that the results will be perfectly amazing!

Other persons respond best to clothespins fastened to the tips of the fingers corresponding to the zones affected (see Figure 14). It is by such simple means that zone therapy brings

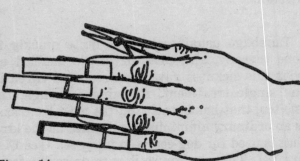

Figure 14.

lasting relief to the sufferings of the human body.

The clothespins may be left on for ten minutes at a time.

Proper massage of the lumbar region reflexes on the feet (see Figure 11) will bring relief to lumbago sufferers. You can be as thorough as tenderness permits.

9

Bladder Problems

Figure 15 will indicate with accuracy the reflex for the bladder. It lies in the lower lumbar region where the reflexes for the rectum and end of the spine are located, but not as deep as those two.

Cystitis, or inflammation of the bladder, is a fairly common disease causing a frequent desire to urinate. Fortunately, this is a condition which responds well to zone therapy on both feet. We recommend massage of the bladder reflex and the extension of this into the kidney reflex, because it is often the uric acid formed in the kidneys that causes the bladder to inflame (see Figure 16).

Press with your thumb into the soft part on the inside of the foot next to the heel pad. There you will find an area about the size of a quarter. Be sure to massage both feet in a similar fashion since we are dealing with zone one; the bladder lies in the middle of the body. Though the massage should be gentle, it should be persistent as well. If you are actually having trouble with your bladder, you should reach a point of pain,

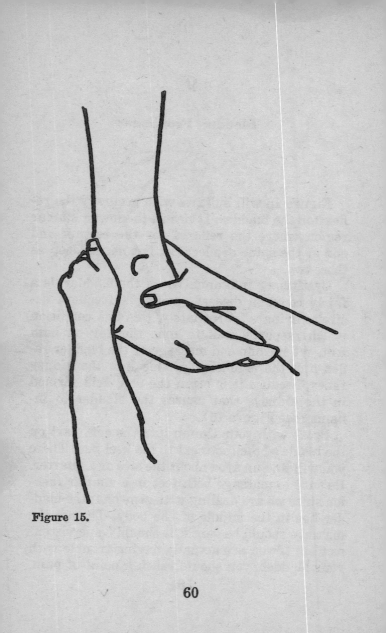

Figure 15.

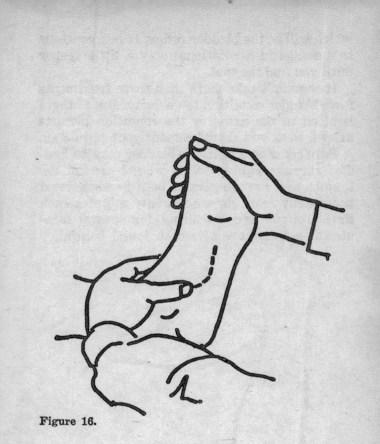

Figure 16.

which will be the bladder reflex. If not, continue to massage in a rotational way a little deeper until you find the spot.

It shouldn't take more than three treatments for a bladder condition to go away. But if there is blood in the urine or the condition persists after a week you should consult your physician.

Pain connected with the bladder may be handled through rubber bands wound around the thumbs and first fingers of both hands several times daily from three to twenty minutes each time. Tongue and lip biting for several minutes at a time have also been found helpful.

10

Blood Pressure

Blood pressure may be lowered by the application of rubber bands to the thumb and first and second fingers of both hands, and by massage of the webs between those fingers and between their joints.

On the other hand, blood pressure may be made to rise by rapidly stroking the entire body for several minutes, morning and night.

In any event, a physician should be consulted.

11

Colds, Sinusitis, Hay Fever

Who has not suffered through the ravages of a cold, emerging a week or so later looking pale and cadaverous? Colds are perhaps mankind's worst irritation, but not even twentieth-century science has been able to solve its riddle. Millions are spent on cold remedies that do little to alleviate the runny noses and sore throats associated with the common cold. So, if that is the case, why not try zone therapy?

There is as much controversy about colds as about how to run the government. Some believe colds are caused by germs attacking the respiratory system and that there is little that the average person can do about them. Others believe that if you take enough vitamin C you can avoid contagion. Still others say that colds are nature's way of cleaning house and eliminating an excess of toxic acid from the system. Be that as it may, we recommend that you suspend general massage of body reflexes and rest your feet, massaging only the toes and the reflexes for the lungs, followed by a short massage of the kidney reflex. Figure 16 shows where the kidneys are located; refer to Figure 4 for the lung reflexes.

The toes were mentioned above because these have to do directly with the sinuses. Congestion of the sinuses is one of the concomitant troubles that come with a bad cold, and congestion is one of the principal causes of trouble in any area. Fortunately, zone therapy works here where even medicines bring only partial relief.

The sinuses being in the head, we must attack the big toe. You should experience tenderness in various parts of the toes and there is where the massage should be applied. There will be a greater amount of pain along the base of the big toe, and you must press this area with two fingers coming from the inner and outer sides of the toe. Persist in this procedure, for the sinus condition won't surrender overnight.

Curiously enough, there is one spot between the second and third toes that appears to have a remarkable connection with the sinuses. If your sinuses are troubling you, experiment, because if you can locate the soreness in that area, a few minutes of massage can bring you relief as few medicines can.

Hay fever reacts to zone therapy treatments in almost all cases, and we urge sufferers of this irritating disorder to apply it to themselves as we shall indicate.

Although the causes of hay fever are as hazy as those for the cold, we know enough of its physical symptoms to state that it creates an acute inflammatory irritation in the nose. A vicious circle is formed whereby the irritation affects the nerves of the area, and these halt the circulation of the blood, causing still more pressure. In Dr. FitzGerald's treatise, he mentions finding a great number of his hay fever patients with somewhat abnormal nose conditions such as bony spurs, protruding turbinate bones, cartilage twisted out of alignment, and the like. He urged such persons to see specialists who could correct these physical conditions as a step toward the control of hay fever itself. He had good luck with applying firm pressure on various points on the roof of the mouth, and he used his thumb for this purpose. It is important to cover the region directly under the nose. The pressure should be maintained for from four to eight minutes at a time, and this should be repeated six or more times daily.

Doctors may want to bring relief to their patients by applying pressure with a cotton-tipped probe on the back wall of the pharynx, as well as directly on the mucous membranes of the nose. The probe may be dipped in trichloracetic acid for a more powerful "punch."

The layman will do well to attack a hay fever condition just as the sinus condition is attacked, by a workout of the reflexes on the big toes.

Other approaches may be tried; since every human being is different, not all approaches work the same, and it is wise to know several alternatives.

Relief has been found by simply pressing the upper lip against the teeth with the forefinger.

Also, a tongue depressor may be applied on the anterior half of the tongue several times a day. Biting the tongue and holding the bridge of the nose firmly between the thumb and forefinger also brings relief. Lastly, clothespins applied to the thumbs and first fingers should affect a hay fever condition.

12

Diabetes

If you will refer to Figure 9, you will see that the pancreas lies between the adrenal glands. Its reflex is a band that extends almost all the way across the left foot and a little over half way on the right foot. Diabetes is a condition brought on by the malfunctioning of the pancreas, so it is this organ that we wish to concentrate upon.

Whereas the reflex for the kidneys moves up the foot, the reflex for the pancreas runs across each foot, just above the kidney reflex. You may have some difficulty determining if you are on the right area, but the general rule applies: where you find soreness and tenderness, massage! (See Figure 17.)

Diabetics must be warned, however, that the reflex massage may induce an increase in the insulin supply, so it is best to discuss the fact that you intend to massage this area with your doctor, as it may be necessary to increase the intake of sugar.

If you work together with your doctor, the urine should be tested carefully during this

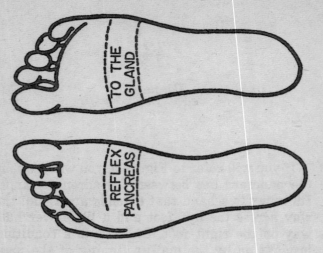

Figure 17.

period. It will be evident that massage in this area might force the liver to throw off some of its excess sugar into the system. If insulin is being used, you will want to continue its use until tests show that a lesser amount can be taken. Your physician will order the decrease, and will be happy to, inasmuch as the use of insulin is not a cure but merely a crutch to the system.

13

Ear Problems, Deafness

The ear is prone to many types of illnesses, so it should be obvious that not all approaches will work the same. This is also borne out by the fact that different parts of the ear involve different zones. We will list various approaches, one of which may just fit your condition and improve your hearing.

One of the handiest methods of curing hearing problems is to place a wad of absorbent lint in the space between the last tooth and the angle of the jaw, so that one is able to bite down hard. Formerly, some dentists would advise their patients to do just that with wonderful results. The "biting" should be prolonged for several minutes, two or three times a day.

Another method that has worked for some people is to squeeze the joints of the ring fingers or the toes corresponding to the ring fingers. There is little one can say to explain this from a scientific point of view, but it has worked where some of the world's greatest ear specialists have failed. In discussions that Dr. FitzGerald had with doctors familiar with zone therapy, he found that nine out of ten cases of otosclerosis or chronic congestion of the membranes of the ear could be improved from 25 to 90 percent following such crude methods.

Ringing of the ears and catarrhal deafness are also improved and sometimes cured by these approaches.

Some cases of deafness have been cured by pressing the teeth of an aluminum comb against the tips of the fingers of the hand (see Figure 18) five minutes at a time, and then following this up with pressure against the floor of the

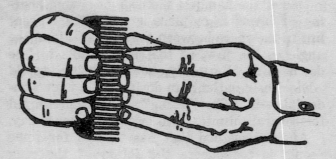

Figure 18.

mouth for six or seven minutes, then against the hard palate, and lastly against the tongue.

In cases of ear trouble, a very wise move is to have the wisdom teeth checked by a dentist. Often ear conditions develop due to a pathological condition of the back teeth.

One of the most effective earache cures we know is to fasten a clothespin for five minutes on the tip of the ring finger.

The most central reflex for the ears on the foot will be found in the area between the third and fourth toes and between the fourth and fifth toes. Tenderness in any such area should be massaged out for general relief of ear problems.

Hearing may generally be improved by the following procedure: Lift the end of the third fingernail of the right hand with the third fingernail of the left hand and do this forcibly for a few minutes at a time. Then do the same with the ring fingers. The same may be done with the middle and fourth toenails of both feet by using the fingernail of the index finger to do the lifting.

14

Epilepsy

Medical science still doesn't know what causes epilepsy; this illness is clouded in mystery, superstition, and even prejudice.

There are recorded cases of lessened epileptic attacks following zone therapy. A person suffering from epilepsy and willing to try zone therapy should experiment with his feet until he discovers areas of tenderness. In most cases, such a person will discover soreness under the big toe, where the reflex of the parathyroid gland is located. If so, proceed with caution, massaging for only a few minutes a day to determine if the attacks can be lessened.

Dr. FitzGerald's treatise speaks of dilatations from eight to ten minutes daily of mouth, nostrils, and external aural canals (packing the outer half of the canal tightly with cotton for a few minutes). He further suggests dilatation of the rectum, the vagina in women, and the urethra in men; for these procedures, medical attention should be sought.

15

Eye Problems

The reflexes to the eyes are found at the bottom of the second and third toes of each foot. It isn't difficult to massage these reflexes, and the way to do it is by a rolling motion done with two fingers. Press down and roll, searching for the sore spot that will indicate you have reached the trouble area, then massage it for a few seconds only.

Sometimes, abnormal eye conditions are caused by taut neck muscles that keep a good supply of blood from reaching the eyes. It is well to massage the top part of the feet, just where the second and third toes begin. The kidneys are also contributory factors in some ailments of the eye, so try massaging the kidney reflexes as well.

The main point of all this massaging is to bring back a healthy circulation of blood to the eyes. Cases of glaucoma have been reported improved by zone therapy; this tends to make sense, inasmuch as glaucoma is caused by the build-up of fluids which harden to produce partial or total blindness. A good blood supply just might inhibit this build-up, and zone therapy will activate circulation.

Eye strain may be relieved by tightly squeezing the knuckles of the first fingers of both hands. With persons whose eyes are especially set apart, this must be repeated on the middle fingers. Apply the pressure on the upper and lower surfaces as well as on the sides. Do this for five minutes at a time.

Sties and such conditions as conjunctivitis and granulated lids are completely relieved by pressure exerted upon the joints of the first and second fingers of the hand corresponding to the diseased eye. Sties can be cleared up in one or two treatments; with other inflammatory conditions, it is necessary to persist for several weeks, treating the eyes to zone therapy three times each week.

Dr. FitzGerald mentions curing patients of inflammation of the optic nerve—a condition which leads to blindness. He did this by applying pressure on the fingers as mentioned and following this by applying pressure with a probe over the inferior dental nerve, where it enters the lower jaw bone; doctors, take notice.

Dr. FitzGerald gives further advice to physicians as follows: "I should like to add that in treating eye strain, conjunctivitis, sties, granulated lids, and eye conditions generally, pressures made with a blunt probe on the muco-cutaneous margins (where the skin joins the mucous membrane in the nostrils) affects the second division of the ophthalmic nerve, and assists materially in bringing about a favorable influence in eye troubles.

"I would also emphasize the importance of seeing that the condition of the eye teeth was perfect, as frequently some chronic inflammatory eye trouble may be caused by an infection from the roots of the canine teeth."

We'd like to sum up by saying that any condition of the eyes brought on by an excess of nerve or muscle tension or faulty circulation can be taken care of by the squeezing of the fingers described earlier. As Dr. FitzGerald put it: "If you don't believe it, try it. It costs nothing but a few minutes' intelligent effort."

16

Fatigue and Depression

Everyone has gone through periods where it seemed impossible to get through the day. Indeed, fatigue is the almost constant companion of large numbers of people in this age of anxiety. People, too, cause their own troubles, by crowding their time with all kinds of activities until they have no time to relax and rest.

Refer to Figure 9. There you will see the reflexes for the all-important glands that should be massaged if you wish to be rid of that feeling of exhaustion. Begin with the most important gland of all, the pituitary, by giving the center of your toe a quick massage, pressing deeply enough to affect this gland. Continue with a massage of the thyroid reflex, and then move on to the adrenal reflexes. Half a minute there will be enough for the pickup you are looking for. After that, tackle the reflex of the sex glands, or gonads, situated in your ankle. No more than fifteen seconds are required for these glands, after which you repeat this procedure on the other foot.

As a final step, you may want to massage the

spleen, producer of red blood cells. This involves the left foot only (see Figure 4). Do it for half a minute and then go back to the pituitary gland reflex and give it a final deep massage of a few seconds' duration. You will notice the difference immediately in your well-being and actual pep.

Depression is closely connected with body fatigue, although we tend to think of it as exclusively mental. The point is that we wouldn't feel depression if our bodily health was up to par. Depression, then, is tied in with fatigue of long duration. To cure it, we suggest the previous massage and, in addition, some attention paid to the pineal gland reflex, which is also located on the big toe. Massage that area as well, since the pineal gland is believed to have a lot to do with organizing the functioning of the endocrine glands.

Continuing mental depression is a sign of psychic problems, and a person suffering from this should seek proper medical attention.

17

Childbirth, Morning Sickness, Menopause, Menstrual Cramps

Women suffer from a wide variety of problems, and it takes a practiced therapist to discover their source. Conditions in many parts of the body may affect the proper functioning of the female organs. Often, the cause of many a trouble is the tension and tightening up of the muscles of the uterus and vagina, and the concomitant nervousness that this will produce.

Trouble with the ovaries can sometimes be traced to a malfunctioning thyroid gland, considered by some as a third ovary. Massage of the thyroid reflex as well as the ovary reflexes will correct such conditions (see Figure 19 for ovary reflex).

On the other hand, if there is hemorrhage, do not use any massage; consult your physician.

Certain functions of the ovaries (and the testes in men) are related to the pituitary gland. They have far-reaching functions in the body and are not connected exclusively with reproductive functions.

The massage of the area above the soles of the feet and under the ankle bone stimulates

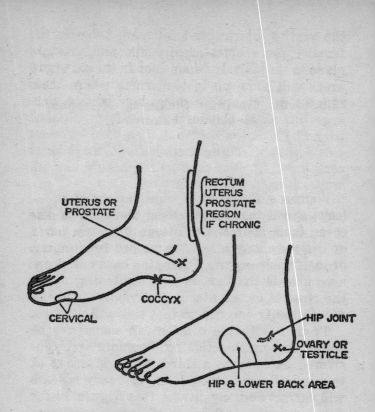

SAME REFLEX AREAS FOUND ON BOTH FEET

Figure 19.

84

the ovaries, uterus, and fallopian tubes in the female, and the testicles, penis, and prostate gland in the male. Inflammation in the sex organ areas will show up in tenderness where these reflexes lie. Figure 20 shows how best to massage this area. Notice that the foot is pulled back and that the thumb is then used to press. Use a gentle, rolling motion for a short time, certainly no longer than half a minute, and always massage the two feet.

The pains of childbirth can be relieved, and the process of labor accelerated by six hours, through zone therapy. The method is simplicity itself; it consists of clasping an aluminum

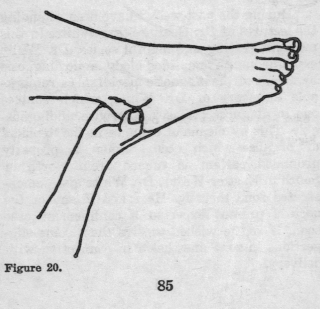

Figure 20.

comb in each hand, as in Figure 13, and holding tight intermittently from the time the contractions begin until delivery. In addition, the soles of the feet should be pressed against some edged surface (a wire brush will do). Rubber bands wound around the big toes and next toes also bring relief.

After-pains are relieved and the expulsion of the after birth is facilitated by stroking the reflex zones in the hands, arms, and legs with an aluminum comb or a wire brush from every ten minutes to half an hour. These assist in the contraction of the uterus.

We must quote a passage from Dr. Fitz-Gerald. He quotes a Dr. R. T. H. Nesbitt, of Waukegan, Illinois, who sent him the following report:

"During the past week I have been attending the lectures of Dr. George Starr White. In this most interesting and helpful series, Dr. White explained and exemplified biodynamic diagnosis by means of the magnetic meridian (a remarkable discovery of Dr. White, which enables one to diagnose diseases otherwise undiagnosable. This by means of changes in the 'tension' of organs—which occurs when a properly grounded patient is turned from North or South to East or West). Dr. White also demonstrated zone therapy. He asked if any of the doctors present expected a confinement case soon. If so, he wished to give them some suggestions in zone anesthesia in connection with delivery.

86

"As I was expecting a call ever hour I told Dr. White, and he gave me some special points concerning this work. Last night I was called to attend what I expected would be my last case in confinement, as I have been doing this work so many years that I intended to retire. From my last night's experience I feel as if I should like to start the practice of medicine all over again.

"The woman I delivered was a primipara (one who had never had a child before, and who, therefore, because of the rigidity of the bones and tissues, has a more difficult labor), small in stature.

"When severe contractions began, and the mother was beginning to be very nervous and complained of pain, at which time I generally administer chloroform, I began pressing on the soles of the feet with the edge of a big file, as I could find nothing else. I pressed on the top of the foot with the thumbs of both hands at the metatarsal-phalangeal joint (where the toes join the foot). I exerted this pressure over each foot for about three minutes at a time. The mother told me that the pressure on the feet gave her no pain whatsoever.

"As she did not have any uterine pain, I was afraid there was no advancement. To my great surprise, when I examined her about ten or fifteen minutes later, I found the head within two inches of the outlet. I then waited about fifteen minutes, and on examination found the head at the vulva. I then pressed again for about one or two minutes on each foot, the edge of the file being on the sole of the foot, and my thumbs over the tarsal-metatarsal joints as before. In this way I exerted pressure on the sole of the foot with the file, and pressure on the dorsum of the foot with my thumbs, doing each foot separately. The last pressure lasted about one and a half minutes on each foot. Within five or ten minutes the head was appearing, and I held it back to preserve the perineum (the tissue joining the vagina and the rectum). It made steady progress, the head and shoulders coming out in a normal manner. Within three minutes the child —which weighed in at 9½ pounds—was born, crying lustily. The mother told me she did not experience any pain whatever, and could not believe the child was born. She laughed and said, 'This is not so bad.'

"Another point that is very remarkable is that after the child was born the woman did not experience the fatigue that is generally felt, and the child was more active than usual. I account for this on the principle that pain inhibits progress of the birth, and tires the child. But as the pain was inhibited, the progress was more steady, and thus fatigue to both mother and child was avoided."

Other equally remarkable cases of painless chilbirth could be given. Aluminum combs to hold in the hands have been tried with success; at such times, a rough-edged box should be placed in the bed so that the patient may be able to press against it with her feet.

Cases of morning sickness may be cured by the use of rubber bands applied on the thumbs and index fingers and by applying pressure on the webs between these fingers.

Hot flashes play an important part in the history of menopause. Women age more rapidly then, and they tend to suffer from insomnia and nervousness. These symptoms can be alleviated by the proper massage of the ovary reflexes, since these will control production of the hormone estrogen. In connection with the massage of the ovary reflexes, there should also be massage of the pituitary gland reflex. Such a practice will enable a woman to go through menopause in a smoother fashion.

Painful menstruation yields like magic to the pressure of a probe aimed at the back wall of the pharynx, but again, we do not recommend that anyone but a physician carry this out. On the other hand, tongue biting is sometimes effective.

For pain in the back or in the thighs, preceding or during menstruation, pressure with the index finger on the back wall of the pharynx will give relief. Also, a tongue depressor may be used to press down on the tongue about three quarters of the way back. This should be done with the help of another person who can hold the patient's head rigid and support the lower jaw. This way the proper amount of pressure

—which should be strong—can be applied. It should last for two minutes, then relaxed and the point of focus changed slightly. Many women who were formerly obliged to go to bed for two or three days each month have been relieved of all distress after a course of this treatment.

Please note that tongue pressure should not be applied in the case of pregnancy.

Lastly, we must note that pressure brought to bear on the thumbs and the first and second fingers of both hands can bring relief of menstrual cramps. Use fingers or clothespins.

18

Gallbladder

Figure 21 indicates where the gallbladder reflex is located. Actually, the gallbladder reflex proper is a bit below and more toward the center of the liver reflex. A little experience will tell you where it is, but you should proceed with caution. Too much massage of the liver reflex can make you quite sick for a while, since it may release a lot of stored-up poisons. It is best to proceed with caution, and massage only a few seconds at a time at first.

The gallbladder is lodged under the right lobe of the liver and is the body's receptacle for bile. It is also the place where gallstones can congregate.

Any tenderness in this area should be massaged carefully. Don't try to massage all the tenderness out in the first try. Zone therapy has helped dissolve gallstone and thus averted painful operations, but it is best not to rush the job.

We do not know if massage of the gallbladder actually dissolves gallstone or simply allows

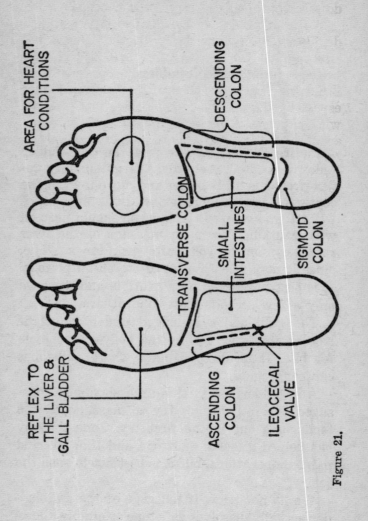

AREA FOR HEART CONDITIONS

DESCENDING COLON

TRANSVERSE COLON

SMALL INTESTINES

SIGMOID COLON

REFLEX TO THE LIVER & GALL BLADDER

ASCENDING COLON

ILEOCECAL VALVE

Figure 21.

92

their passage through and out, but it certainly does something to alleviate the condition.

We might mention here, since the gallbladder is so interconnected with the liver, that massage of the liver reflex will sometimes remedy chronic lack of energy in a person. This is an area that is certainly worth checking out, especially if you detect tenderness. Just proceed with caution. After a while, if the liver responds, you may massage longer and more thoroughly.

Rubber bands on the thumbs, first and second fingers, and comparable toes will have a beneficial effect on the gallbladder and may be tried without fear of a liver reaction.

19

Goiter

Goiter used to be quite a prevalent condition, although it seemed to vary from place to place, some areas being more conducive to it than others. Nowadays, a great deal more is known about the thyroid gland and the use of iodine in the system, so enlargement of the thyroid is rare.

In the first part of this century, when Dr. Fitzgerald was writing and working, goiters were a bothersome malady, but he had learned how to deal with them thanks to zone therapy; he did so by the use of probes passed through the nostrils and applied to the back wall of the pharynx. He also insisted on placing rubber bands around the thumb, first and second fingers, and sometimes even the ring finger, keeping them there for ten or fifteen minutes at a time three or four times daily.

20

Headaches, Migraine

Instead of using aspirin and other highly touted pills for headaches—which are taken by the millions, with unimaginable after-effects—people should follow zone therapy for relief, for nothing could be simpler and less harmful.

If the headache is due to neuralgia or nervous strain, the best remedy is to press your thumb or something like a spoon against the roof of the mouth, as nearly as possible under the part that hurts. The pressure should be maintained for from three to five minutes, no less. If the headache is extensive, you may have to shift the pressure to cover the rest of the roof of the mouth.

These points of pressure may extend from the roots of the front teeth, for a frontal headache, to the junction of the soft and hard palates when the headache lies in the back of the head. Likewise, from one side of the mouth to the other if the headache is located to one side of the head.

If the headache is caused by other conditions, the case gets a little more complicated. For instance, there are headaches caused by poisons caused by improper bowel movements, constipation, too many drinks the night before, or eye-strain. Little help will be obtained from the above method in these cases.

On the other hand, headaches frequently respond to pressure exerted over the joints of the thumb or fingers. Dr. White once cured a woman patient who had suffered from a headache for three weeks by firmly pressing the first, second, and third fingers of her hands.

The best approach when a headache is due to eye-strain is to relax the neck area by massaging the entire big toe in the following manner: Take it between two fingers and rotate it right and left, round and round until relief comes.

If you know that a specific organ is causing your headache (the stomach or liver, for example), work the big toe as indicated and then work on the reflex to that organ.

Many other headaches are cured by massaging the connecting spot between the big toe and the next toe. You might notice a tenderness there, or might search for it, because some headaches don't give up unless that zone is massaged. Even migraine will yield to the right spot between the toes. Look for it, for in some people it may be located between two other toes!

21

Heart Disorders

Heart failure can be prevented through zone therapy, and we would like to discuss this now at some length. No one will argue the fact that the heart is one of the most important organs in the body; it is a strong muscle, capable of working night and day for a lifetime without presenting its owner with the least bit of trouble. But we tend to take advantage of a good thing; we abuse it and then wonder why it gives us trouble. Zone therapy can tell you just how much you have been leaning on your heart, and it is important that you learn to work the heart reflex so that you can engage in the proper preventive measures. See Figure 22 for the right way to massage this all-important reflex. You will notice how the thumb presses in on the pad of the little toe. The heart is not that small an organ, so you may massage the area with some degree of certainty. Any tenderness there is an indication of some degree of congestion, which, if allowed to continue unchecked for some time, could lead to heart attack.

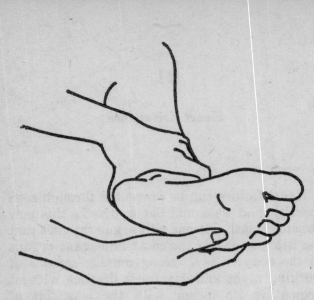

Figure 22.

The heart and the muscles directly connected to it are located slightly to the left of the chest cavity, so that the reflex to this all-important organ is to be found in the second, third, and fourth zones of the left foot (see Figure 23 for correct position for massaging the heart reflex).

Tenderness in this area may be an indication of congestion and this could lead, in the long run, to a heart attack. Now since the heart is well buried in the chest cavity, it will be necessary for you to apply strong pressure to reach the right reflex. Use the front of the thumb, and the nail as well.

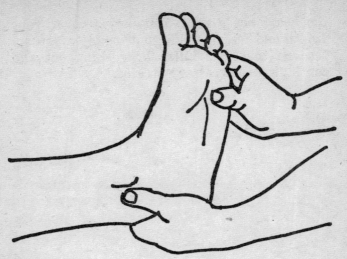

Figure 23.

No matter what your trouble may be, you can aid your heart through zone therapy. Sometimes, massaging the heart reflex will lead to a sensation of pain shooting from the foot to the heart, but this is followed by a good feeling and it means that the heart has been aided.

With angina pectoris, where pains shoot up the shoulder and arm, you must work over a wide area of reflexes, from the base of the little toe and the third and fourth toes down to the center of the heart reflex. The shoulder pains may be aided by massaging the little toe itself.

One note of warning must be uttered. Sometimes if the pains disappear, a person is apt to take up where he left off. But remember that

101

the heart needs rest. You may recover your health and feel fit to kill, but too often you are the one that gets killed by rushing out and continuing unnecessary strains.

22

Hemorrhoids

Hemorrhoids are those extremely painful veins that have become congested and protrude from the rectum. Not only are they a great inconvenience, but they sometimes bleed and require surgical care.

Zone therapy can work wonders with hemorrhoids, dissipating the pain that accompanies them. Apply yourself to their reflexes as shown in Figure 23. Here is how to do it: Instead of a rolling type of massage, press in towards the bone and down towards the heel, firmly. Do this all the way around the heel, using the thumb for one side and the index finger for the other. Be sure to apply plenty of pressure and do this on both feet. Recheck for specific sore spots and massage those a little longer than the rest of the reflex. At first you may have trouble in finding any soreness whatever, but that is because you may not be pressing hard enough. Move the flesh of the heel back and forth against the bone until you find the tenderness; if you suffer from hemorrhoids, it will be there.

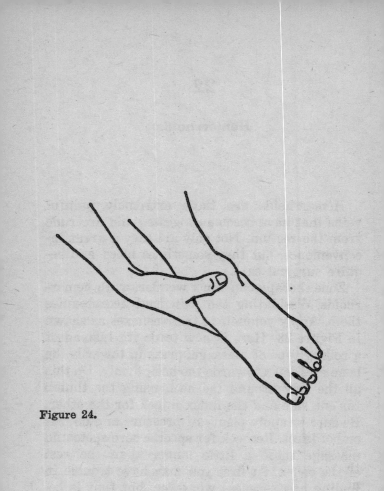

Figure 24.

23

Hiccoughs

The founding fathers of zone therapy found several marvelous ways to deal with this little malady. Dr. FitzGerald, in his usual charming manner, describes one method as follows: "For, when we grasp the tongue of the hiccougher, and with a long pull, a strong pull, and a pull all together, haul the offending member to tongue's length—and hold it there—we cure the spasmodic contraction of the diaphragm (the cause of the hiccough) by influencing the zone in which the trouble originates."

Other methods include interlocking all the fingers of the hands firmly and holding them there, exerting as much pressure as possible; applying clothespins to the tips of the thumbs and fingers; and, lastly, applying pressure on the tongue with a tongue depressor, right in the middle. Good luck!

24

Infections, Lymph Glands, Kidneys

Infections can occur anywhere on the body if the skin has been broken and foreign objects have penetrated. It is a good idea to keep the lymph glands in shape by massaging their reflex in the feet, for it is the lymph glands that take the main burden of fighting infection throughout the body.

These lymph glands compose an entire network of vessels that collect fluids seeping through the walls of blood vessels. This material collects at specific nodes in the armpits, in the groin, and all around the neck. It is calculated that there are between six and seven hundred nodes in the body. Figure 25 indicates their location as a reflex in the foot, and the way to message this reflex.

The whole area on top of the foot should be massaged, from one side of the ankle bone to the other. Use as many fingers as you find convenient, or the whole of the thumb, pressing and circling. Be sure to massage both feet.

If you will refer to Figure 11 you will see just where the kidney reflexes are located.

Figure 25.

Since the kidneys have the job of ridding the entire organism of accumulated poisons, normal and abnormal, you will understand why we suggest that you go easy on them at first. There can be such a thing as overmassaging the kidney reflexes at the beginning, when they are not used to it and are overloaded with poisons. If the reflexes are tender, proceed slowly and do not massage more than a minute each day for the first few days.

As we have already mentioned, the kidneys may affect the eyes, so in cases of eye-strain, try massaging the kidney reflexes.

Severe infections should logically involve massage of the lymph gland reflexes and the kidney reflexes as well.

25

Insomnia

This mysterious malady that comes and goes like a curse, without your knowing why or how, can be controlled by one of several methods, all vouched for by Dr. FitzGerald and Dr. Bowers.

The first approach is to interlock all the fingers of the two hands for no less than ten minutes, pressing as hard as you can stand it.

The second method is to stroke your forearms on all their surfaces with a wire brush, or, if no wire brush is available, with your fingernails. This is to be carried on for five or ten minutes.

Lastly, you may press with your thumb and index finger above the bridge of the nose, holding that position for ten minutes.

26

Joint Pains

Sometimes we wake up in the morning with vague pains across the back of the neck and shoulders. The best way to relieve this kind of tension is to press strongly with the knuckles of your hand against the sole of the foot, while with the fingers of the other hand you dig in and try to loosen the ligaments and muscles across the top of the foot directly above the area you are working with your knuckles.

Body joints will tend to ache where there is any tendency to broken metatarsal arches. Our advice is to see a foot specialist who will recommend the right kind of shoes to buy in order to correct this condition. The difference this will make in your everyday energy is astounding.

Leg cramps can be disposed of by the simple expedient of massaging the cords in back of the knee. Try that next time you are semi-paralyzed from a cramp.

Remember that in zone therapy the knee corresponds with the elbow, and the hip with the shoulder of the same side. Firm manipulation of the joints of the thumbs, fingers, hand, elbow, and shoulder affect positively the corresponding joints in the lower extremity. You may pull, flex, extend, and rotate the various parts at the same time that you apply pressure, holding various positions for a few seconds.

After you have treated the hand or wrist, compare it with the other hand and wrist for lightness and flexibility and then see if you notice any difference in the feet. It may take you a while to catch these differences, but the connections are surely there.

If you treat these zones this way you may find yourself rid of aches and pains, and much relaxed.

27

Nervousness

Nervousness is a condition endemic to contemporary living, and of course different people deal with it in different ways. You can take pills, tranquilizers, and thus function. Or, if you have the money, you can go to a psychiatrist and go into the problem at length.

Zone therapy cannot help you if the causes are psychic disturbances, but for that occasional feeling of butterflies in your stomach or a particularly difficult period of adjustment to a new job or a new mate, here are some simple, workable methods of reducing tension:

From a preventive point of view, you might try the ten minute daily toning-up exercises listed in the last chapter of this book. However, if you are presently in the throes of a nervous attack, try placing rubber bands on the first, second, and third fingers of both hands and, if that is not enough, on the respective toes as well.

Clenching of the hands for prolonged periods is extremely relaxing and is highly recommended for the nervous system; it should be done while the jaws are firmly set against each other. The interlocking of the fingers of both hands is another method that works just as well, and is something that we do instinctively in times of stress or shock, when emotions are at their peak.

The best suggestion is to take a wire brush and brush the entire body with it, from the fingertips to the tips of the toes. Do it for five minutes in the morning and then again before retiring for the night.

Some people, in manifesting extreme anger, will bite their lip, sometimes hard enough to bleed. The majority, as we have said, will clench their hands and double up their toes in their shoes. Nobody has come up with a reason for it, but we do it and will continue to do it involuntarily and automatically because such actions relieve pain and nervous tension. They produce an actual form of analgesia similar to that which follows the injection of an anesthetic into a sensory nerve.

So people who scoff at zone therapy are not paying attention to what the body itself is telling them. Dr. FitzGerald certainly believed in it, and was patient enough to work at it for several months in some cases. He cites the case of a woman with writer's cramp caused by her nervousness. She suffered so much from it that she couldn't hold a pen and was unable to sleep at night. It took him months to cure her, but he did it. And it was done by using an aluminum comb and combing the front and back of her hands and her fingertips, and pressing her tongue down with a tongue depressor for four or five minutes a day.

28

Neuralgia

Reference to Figures 6 and 7 should tell you in which zone the pain lies and will therefore guide you as to how best to attack the condition through the feet reflexes. Most often, neuralgia will yield to pressure on thumbs, fingers, or toes of the zones involved, but we suggest that a doctor be consulted in the event that there is an infection of the teeth or something similar.

Dr. FitzGerald also suggests packing the outer third of the aural canal tightly with slightly moistened cotton.

He mentions a case of another doctor friend of his, Dr. Roemer, who treated a patient with trifacial neuralgia of two years' standing. Nothing had helped this man; his attacks were often of four and five days' duration, at which times he was unable to speak. Speech brought him paroxysms of pain that radiated over the entire left side of his face, from the lower to the upper jaw and up into the left eye, leaving him limp as a rag.

Dr. Roemer applied rubber bands on the joints nearest the tip of the thumb and forefinger of the left hand. In less than ten minutes the patient was talking and laughing. His advice to the man was to apply the bands for half an hour if another attack came on.

29

Neuritis

Neuritis can be extremely painful and crippling. Cases of neuritis of the shoulder, for instance, are reported after a person has suffered a hard fall and injured that extremity. Bones may not be broken, but the nerves are neverthelesss affected and, in due time, pain builds and builds until it is so severe that the person cannot move the limb at all.

Obviously, in a condition such as that, you must find the reflex area in the foot and go to work, carefully at first since the pain in the foot will be intense! It is best to work for a minute or two and then rest, but a twenty-minute workout would not be too unusual if you want to make progress. In cases of shoulder problems you will work below the little toe. It might take as long as a week but results will come (see Figure 24).

Dr. FitzGerald cured a man suffering from neuritis of the arm and shoulder for six years by clamping clothespins on the fingers of the affected arm for twelve minutes, after which the man was able to raise his arm over his head for the first time. Following a few weeks' treatment of five-minute applications of tight rubber bands around the ends of his fingers, the man reported himself cured.

Sciatic neuritis can be helped with deep pressure from the teeth of an aluminum comb upon the toes.

30

Paralysis, Strokes

Apoplexy, or the type of stroke caused by a blood clot in the brain, is in turn caused by a hemorrhage somewhere in the brain. It usually affects one side of the body, the side opposite to where the clot in the brain is located. The paralysis may be complete or partial.

The paralysis is brought about by the pressure which the clot brings to bear on that part of the brain controlling the motor action of the part of the body paralyzed. The nervous impulses governing action cannot be transmitted and thus the muscles cannot move.

Paralysis may or may not be incurable, depending on the location of the clot, its size, the health of the individual, and the capacity of the organism to begin absorbing the clot. If the clot begins to be absorbed, it will allow the brain to once again begin transmitting messages through to the afflicted part.

How can zone therapy work in a case like this? It pays to go back and realize that the cause of this paralysis is more often than not high blood pressure. That is the real culprit, so it behooves us to check and see if the kidneys, liver, and other organs are doing their part the way they should. This should not be difficult once you understand foot reflexes and how they respond. For whatever is really behind this condition will respond with marked tenderness. This is the first step, and it might take some time to remove the cause of it. But it makes sense, doesn't it, that by removing the obstacles in the way of proper blood circulation you are doing for your body what it really needs done to get on the road to health.

To assist the brain directly to get over the condition, you must tackle the brain reflexes in the big toe. Some of the reflexes cross behind the neck, so that if the right side of the body has been paralyzed we must work on the toe of the left foot. If any part of this toe is tender, massage it out, thus assisting the circulation of blood in the brain. It won't hurt to massage the toe on the side afflicted as well, to benefit the entire brain.

31

Pneumonia

Nobody plays with pneumonia; it is a very serious condition in which the lungs or the bronchial tubes are acutely inflamed due to either a virus, bacterial attack, or other causes such as aspiration of foreign material into the lungs. The first thing that zone therapy can do is alleviate the congestion and relieve tension by massaging the reflexes for shoulders and lungs.

Dr. FitzGerald was keen on rubber bands on all fingers or toes or on both, plus tongue pressure with tongue depressor and the use of a cotton-tipped probe on appropriate zones of the mouth, pharynx, and nose.

Reflex massage of the lung areas in both feet will benefit the bronchial tubes, but bear in mind that the massage should be deep. Start under the big toe, in the same place where the throat reflexes are located, so you cover the entire respiratory apparatus. Press in with the thumb into the soft area under the toe and massage all the way down to the end of the pad, moving with a pressing yet circular motion.

With fever, be sure to cover the pituitary gland reflex as well.

32

Prostate Problems

The prostate gland lies directly in front of the rectum, so the reflexes will be the same for the prostate and the rectum. The prostate is the largest male sex gland, and it circles the neck of the urethra as it emerges from the bladder. Its location, for our purposes, is in the first zone of both feet.

An enlargement of this gland—that is, any amount of congestion—will cause great pain and inconvenience when it comes to voiding urine. As it also affects the nervous system, it is important to keep it functioning properly.

Any indisposition of this gland will result in the reflex being quite tender, perhaps extending down to the lower portion of the inside of the heel, in the direction of the bladder reflex (see Figure 26).

Fortunately, zone therapy can get this gland back to health in a relatively short time. Note the position of the hand (Figure 27) in massaging this area, and how the thumb presses one side above the heel while the knuckle of the forefinger presses from the other side, aided

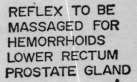

REFLEX TO BE
MASSAGED FOR
HEMORRHOIDS
LOWER RECTUM
PROSTATE GLAND

Figure 26.

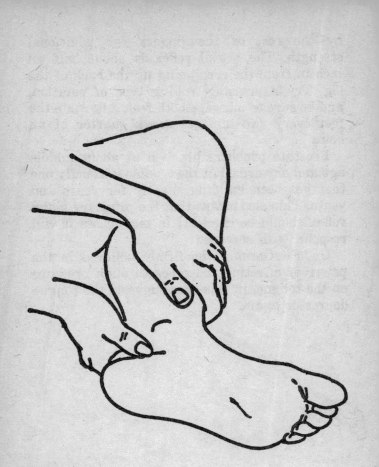

Figure 27.

by the rest of the fingers for additional strength. The actual reflex is about half an inch in from the cord going up the back of the leg. Try a pressing, rolling type of rotation, and be sure to massage both feet. Alternate the feet every two minutes for a quarter of an hour.

Prostate problems hit men at about middle age and onwards, but the trouble is usually one that has been building silently for years and years. This also means that the pituitary gland reflex should be checked; in most cases it will respond with soreness.

Dr. FitzGerald, who firmly believed in the power of affecting the zones through pressure on the tongue, in this case suggests the tongue depressor again.

33

Rectum Disorders, Prolapsed Rectum

We have seen that the reflex to the rectum, prostate, and hemorrhoids is one and the same, with hemorrhoids logically at the heel.

Rectal problems may be large or small. If large, they may extend, as far as reflexology is concerned, as far as three to four inches up from the heel. Proceed as with the massage for bladder problems, bending the foot back as far as possible, stretching the cord immediately beneath the skin and tackling the flesh to the inside of it. When you have worked out some of the tenderness from the area, go back and massage the cord itself. It may be agony because the inflammation of the rectum will have provided its reflex with enough tenderness for the massage to be anything but fun, but grit your teeth and bear down because the results will pay big dividends.

Often, as a person gets older, a condition known as a prolapsus or prolapsed rectum sets in. This is nothing but the gradual and very painful and uncomfortable protruding of the rectum, and it is usually accompanied by its acute inflammation and swollen condition. Apply here the same approach as for hemorrhoids; the results will no doubt amaze you!

34

Relaxation

Interlocking the fingers of the hand and squeezing for all you are worth is about the oldest and best way there is to relax, if you can manage to do it for more than a few minutes at a time. If you are serious about it, however, and do just what we tell you, you will discover that no matter how rough and rotten a day you have had, a soothing feeling will steal all over your body and your cares will seem to dissolve in consequence. If you tire of the first approach, you may switch to applying firm pressure on finger and thumb tips. Clothespins are marvelous for this therapy because once you have applied them you can forget them and even take a nap. You will awaken a different person!

Another approach, mentioned before, is the setting of the jaws by biting down hard and keeping the pressure constant. This may be facilitated by taking a piece of rubber or cloth and biting on it instead. If there is no one around to make fun of you while you're at it, try stretching your lips outward, for as many minutes as you can stand it. It works!

35

Rheumatism

First off, we might mention that rheumatism is one of those mysterious ailments that science hasn't gotten around to solving yet. It attacks thousands and thousands of people and there is very little that they can do . . . unless they know zone therapy.

Dr. FitzGerald had a hunch, which he set down for whatever it was worth, that offending corns, warts, and bitten fingernails may be responsible for rheumatic conditions. Is that the case with you? Does your rheumatism go hand in hand with any of those little-suspected happenings?

He mentions a peculiar case of his in which a patient, suffering from rheumatism of the left shoulder and arm, had been unable to sleep for more than three weeks on account of the pain. But he had a small callus on the tip of his left thumb that corresponded to the zone where his pain was located. When the callus was removed and pressure with a comb applied to the area, the man was cured within four days!

Rheumatism responds to zone therapy. Treat the zones involved and the pain will begin to disappear. Apply rather hard massage twice a day to the zone involved, on both feet or one as the case may be.

36

Sciatica

The old medical sages of zone therapy suggested, first off, that you look for an infection in the mouth or elsewhere, holding that the third molar teeth were often responsible.

One of the key sensitive areas in sciatica, in the hand, is the junction of hand and wrist, in the palmar surface. Press tightly with an aluminum comb.

Sciatic neuritis has been cured with deep pressure by an aluminum comb on the fleshy part of the toes as well as on the fingers. If the pain is severe in the back of the legs, use the comb to apply pressure on the sole of the foot. If the pain occurs in the front part of the legs, the top of the foot should be pressed with the comb. However, the best and most rapid relief for sciatica is obtained by attacking the soles of the feet. In fact, Dr. White even "invented" a device consisting of a piece of hard wood about five inches in length cut with deep screw-like threads. He had a hole drilled through it and a rope inserted, so that the patient could use it with a strong pull for five and ten minutes at a time, several times a day.

If sciatica is due to hip dislocation, zone therapy may not be as favorable. A twisting of the hip or subluxation of the hip joint may be a condition best treated by your doctor or chiropractor. But try zone therapy first!

Look at it this way: The sciatic nerve is the biggest nerve in the body, three-quarters of an inch wide. Coming out of the pelvis, it descends along the back of the thigh and later divides into two. If this big nerve ever gets inflamed, you are obviously in for a lot of pain. And the causes may be many, not just your dislocated hip. It may be due to an injury sustained in quite another part of the body, to an inflamed prostate gland, to constipation, or to a misplacement of the vertebra. Look at Figure 28 for the proper way to massage the reflex to this important nerve and try using the eraser end of a good pencil.

The reason for the pencil is that this is a deeply buried reflex and only a fairly sharp instrument is going to reach it. Please notice that the reflex will be found back from the center of the heel pad, toward the outside of the foot.

Massage with a deep, rolling action, doing your best to forget the intense pain that it might bring if the right spot has been located. There have been people who have found a cure for their pain in one or two treatments, but

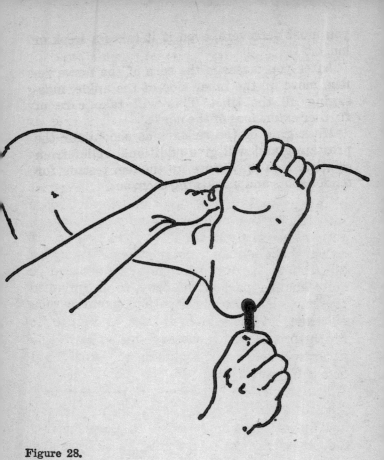

Figure 28.

you must persevere, even if it takes a week or longer.

After you massage the core of the nerve reflex, move up the inner side of the ankle, massaging all the time. This will take care of further extensions of the nerve.

Massaging of the reflexes as shown for the prostate gland will give additional relief from sciatica. You may move up the leg, testing for tender spots and massaging them out.

37

Sore Throat, Loss of Voice

The next time you suffer from a sore throat, try zone therapy instead of sweetened cough pills.

The fleshy part of your big toe is where you will locate the reflex to your throat and, since the pain is in the front part, you will want to massage the top of the toe, just where it merges with your foot. Grab it between your thumb and forefinger and see if it doesn't respond with tenderness the minute you apply some pressure. That should be your tell-tale sign.

The congestion in your throat may be caused by an excessive amount of poison in your system, and if that is the case, that condition will have to be cleared first before you can obtain relief. On the other hand, if you are just catching a cold, you may be surprised at what the proper massage can do for you.

And not only a sore throat but a stiff neck will yield to this approach.

Loss of voice may be helped by using a napkin or handkerchief to grasp the tongue, and pulling it slowly but firmly out and in all directions.

38

Stomach Disorders

One of the worst things that can befall the stomach is the perforation of its internal lining, and the subsequent pain and danger posed by such a condition. Ulcers may be caused by many things; bad food, greasy and hastily eaten, as well as by negative emotional states of being, such as fear and anger. That there is a direct relationship between digestion and the emotions is well known and can be felt by every individual: the butterflies caused by fear and anxiety, the heavy feeling caused by depression, the cramps after undue tension. Something has to be done about the emotions if a cure is going to be effected, but zone therapy can be a powerful aid in bringing back the health of your stomach.

Since the stomach lies fairly high in the abdomen (not far down, as most people think) and somewhat to the left, we can form a pretty good idea of the location of its reflexes in the human foot. Please refer to Figure 11 for the exact area. Begin to explore the area with your thumb or the knuckle of your index finger;

some spots may be more tender than others because the organ is fairly large. Some spots may be really painful, an indication that trouble is brewing. You must then massage that area as softly as you can, increasing the pressure as you see that you can bear the temporary pain. You might be surprised at how quickly stomach troubles react to zone therapy, but you shouldn't be; there are a tremendous number of arteries and veins feeding that area, so that the response to increased circulation can be very vigorous.

Gastric ulcers will respond to firm pressure in the wrists. The front or back of the wrist, if sore, will signify ulcers either in the anterior or the posterior stomach wall. Massage until pain disappears, morning and night. If the ulcer is causing acute pain, try firm pressure on the appropriate fingers for three to fifteen minutes.

The last applies to any abdominal pain, such as that caused by indigestion.

In cases of vomiting, try scratching the thumb and index fingers of the left hand and the first three fingers of the right hand, as well as the webs in between those fingers; also the corresponding sections of the foot.

39

Testes

The reflex to the testes, found below the area marked for the prostate gland in Figure 26, will yield to massage in case of injury or obstruction.

An infection should be treated by reflex massage twice daily until cleared. Dr. FitzGerald emphasizes tongue biting, as it affects all zones and can have an ameliorating effect on any constriction. Rubber bands on all fingers will work just as well.

40

Varicose Veins, Leg Cramps

Zone therapy specialists have found that varicose veins have a connection with the liver and, therefore, they treat the liver reflex in the foot when faced with varicose conditions. The same goes for leg cramps. It is necessary to proceed with some caution at first, since we do not want to activate the liver so much that it releases too many pent-up poisons at one time. Start by massaging the reflex in the right foot for a few seconds morning and night, sensing the degree of tenderness and comparing it to the tenderness the next day. It should decrease slowly, and as it does, the massage can be a little more extensive.

Varicose veins in the rectum have been discussed under the subject of hemorrhoids. All of these are conditions which yield to the proper use of zone therapy.

41

Preventive Therapy—Ten Minutes A Day To Health

Proper and plentiful circulation is the key to health. Your blood just has to get to all parts of the body if it is to remove the many poisons that are secreted by each and every living cell, let alone remove the many dead cells. Modern man does not exercise enough, and when he does, it is through specialized movements that do not take care of every section and muscle of his body. This is the cause of much disease in our time, and it isn't helped by diets too rich in sugars and processed starches and carbohydrates.

There is no substitute for exercise and good dietary habits. But if these rules are observed, and you also take it upon yourself to exercise your glands through zone therapy for just ten minutes a day, we can practically promise you a long, happy life free from the many physical troubles that we see each and every day.

We won't go into the matters of diet and exercise, since such matters would take us too far afield of our purpose in this book. But you have been warned. And let us say that as far as exercise is concerned, many authorities believe the best possible exercise in the world is a good long walk each day. Be sure to carry nothing in your hands. If such a walk can be taken with bare feet on the sandy shore of a sea or a lake, you may be sure that nature itself is doing your zone therapy for you!

But form the habit of rising ten minutes earlier than usual each morning, and of sitting down with your feet up during that time, massaging each and every major reflex we have talked about in this book, with special attention to the areas that are sensitive: those are your future trouble spots.

Begin with your toes and work down to the large pads of the front part of your foot. Don't forget the spine reflex and the various reflexes for the glands, waiting to be brought to maximum performance by this simple expedient. After all, you can exercise your muscles by engaging in a sport, but where is the exercise for for any specific gland? These marvelous structures are supposed to go through life functioning at peak capacity, without the least attention. Unless they go on strike! Then and only then do you start to worry and run to doctors. But why wait, sometimes till it's too late, when a few minutes a day can see you through with buoyant health?

Start the good habit today. If we have done nothing in the writing of this book but convince you of the necessity of exercising your glands through zone therapy then we have succeeded, and your life will take a turn for the better. Good luck, and happy massaging!

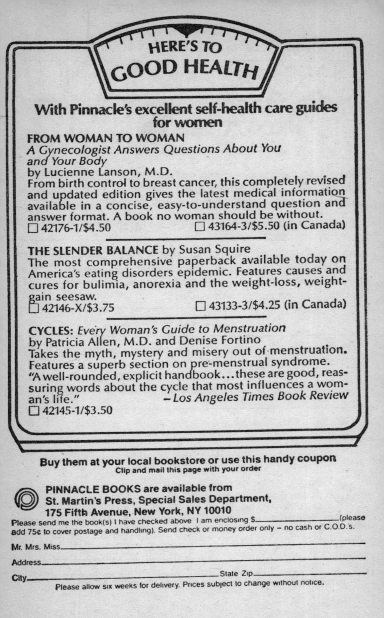

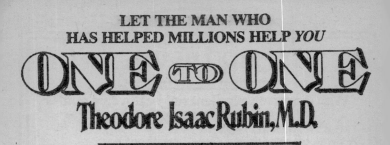